The Courtiers of Civilization

The Courtiers
of Civilization

A STUDY OF DIPLOMACY

Sasson Sofer

Cover art: *Departure of the Ambassadors* (1497–1498) by artist Vittore Carpaccio.

Published by State University of New York Press, Albany

For information, contact State University of New York Press, Albany, NY
www.sunypress.edu

Production by Ryan Morris
Marketing by Anne Valentine

Library of Congress Cataloging-in-Publication Data

Sofer, Sasson.
  The courtiers of civilization : a study of diplomacy / Sasson Sofer.
     pages ; cm
  Includes bibliographical references and index.
  Summary: "Comprehensive study of the diplomat and the diplomatic mission in western civilization"—Provided by publisher.
  ISBN 978-1-4384-4893-0 (hardcover : alk. paper) 1. International relations. 2. Diplomacy. I. Title.
  JZ1305.S663 2013
  327.2–dc23
                                           2013000112

10   9   8   7   6   5   4   3   2   1

*To the memory of my
beloved brother, Fathi*

Contents

Preface

A T THE CENTER of this study of diplomacy stands its principal protag-
onist—the professional diplomat. Our main purpose is to evaluate
anew the portrait and the reputation of the diplomatic envoy in Western
society. We consider the following three constitutive propositions: first,
that practice was always central to the evolution of diplomatic culture;
second, that the nature of diplomacy, which is inherently stable, may
withstand the challenges of contemporary international politics; and
last, that diplomatic practice is embedded within an "ethical-pluralist"
tendency and is fundamentally intertwined with diplomatic competence.

The "diplomat" is one of the most vilified and ridiculed persona in
the history of international affairs, as well as in literary works. The sus-
picions, the criticism, and the bias directed against diplomats are old as
the profession itself. There is, indeed, no other civil servant so closely
associated with adjectives such as "failure" and "decline." The portrayal
of diplomats as timid and incompetent is related, first and foremost, to
their close association with power. In this regard, diplomats are the victims of their vocation. The dim view taken of diplomats is quite striking
in comparison with that of statesmen, sovereigns, and captains of war.
Diplomats' presumed social privileges, and essential diplomatic virtues,
such as moderation and truthfulness, have repeatedly cast them as chosen scapegoats.

Diplomats' political weakness, but also the fundamental misunderstanding of the essence of diplomacy, impede and hamper their ability
to be efficient moral agents of international society. Diplomats' political dependence and obedience are hardly enough to save them from
public wrath. On the contrary, their detachment and reserve, which are

essential for success, open the way for the accusation that they are merely executioners of orders. There is, it seems, an incompatibility between the moral essence of diplomacy, and the ignominious place allocated to its practitioners. Ultimately, they may succumb to a Byzantine fate, where their lives and the welfare of the state are two divergent considerations.

Diplomacy could have been emancipatory, and more constructive in its achievements. Instead, it has been relegated to a secondary place in international politics. This study attempts to construct a more coherent, and implicitly more favorable, profile of professional diplomats than emerges from their popular image.

Diplomacy is neither a preconceived idea, nor an abstract construct. It was originated and ordained in the necessity to conduct relations among separate political entities in a civilized way. At its best, diplomacy was capable of overcoming prejudices, and moderating international conflicts. Good diplomacy, observed the diplomat and poet Alexis Saint-Léger, is "imagination, foresight, suggestion, representation, execution." Diplomacy is a unique social encounter, with an inclination toward the peaceful and the consensual. It has a civilizational standing, as exemplified by its origins in different cultures, and at different periods in history. If the essence of diplomacy is still valid, then much is to be gained from the classical writings of philosophers and practitioners, from Rosier to Satow and Nicolson.

— ••• —

Diplomacy's place within international theory is rather precarious. The attempt to construct a diplomatic theory of international relations may prove inconclusive at present, especially since international theory, in all its approaches and schools, is currently immersed in one of its deepest crises. The intellectual uncertainty that has prevailed since the end of the Cold War era has brought about a certain fruition in the search for new concepts and methods, but theoretical refinement was not enough to cope with the accelerating pace of change taking place in the world order. Certainly, abandoning diplomacy in international theory would constitute a failure, not supported by any valid methodological or theoretical principles. Though they complain about the intellectual paucity of diplomatic study, theorists have not been able to integrate diplomacy in a meaningful way into their theoretical frameworks, nor to significantly enhance our understanding of international reality.

Methodologically, this study is interdisciplinary, relying on historical evidence, sociological analysis, and, where appropriate, political thought. It is substantially based to a great extent on reading classical diplomatic texts from the late Renaissance to the last century. We consider the writings of diplomatists to be an important source, despite their laudatory, even narcissistic tone. There is also much to be gained from sociological scholarship. The writings of, for instance, Georg Simmel and Norbert Elias, provide profound insights into the social properties of the diplomatic encounter, and on the concepts of social distance and estrangement. Indeed, the pluralistic approach is most appropriate for the study of diplomacy, further augmenting the merits of the English School.

It is often asked, even by serious scholars, Who are the diplomats? The inclusive approach that regards representatives of NGOs and even ordinary citizens as legitimate competitors with diplomats, is gaining momentum. Formerly, diplomats were regarded as such only on the basis of their rank and prerogatives, as defined by international conventions. As diplomatic envoys they conduct their business according to a distinctive code of behavior. They labor to preserve what has been achieved, and aspire for what is attainable in international politics. But, when so instructed they may act also as emissaries of change.

Professional diplomacy is a way of life, from apprenticeship to retirement. The diplomat moves within a bounded social milieu, is schooled by his country's foreign ministry, and rewarded by assignments and promotions. As an envoy he faces risks and hazards on several fronts—the ups and downs of a career dominated by a bureaucracy bifurcated between home and abroad, the whims of his political masters, and the existential danger of being merely the symbolic representative of his country. The nomadic life, and the demands of diplomatic rituals, make diplomacy the craft of strangers. But in a dialectical way, being a stranger serves diplomats well in their roles as negotiators and reporters.

Diplomatic credentials are formally granted by international law, while the substantive ones depend on the diplomat's talents and ethics. Diplomats are experts in precise and accurate communication, whether oral or written. More attention should be paid, in this regard, to the natural symbiosis between literature and diplomacy. Accomplished writers and poets have served as successful practitioners. Diplomats perform on a variety of stages—palaces, dining halls, hotel lobbies, and even spas and cemeteries. Under mutual agreements, such places become public spheres, demarcated and ordained as diplomatic forums. As masters of changing settings, diplomats undeservedly gained a dubious reputation of their character—honorable spies, timid appeasers, and dull bureaucrats.

In fact, diplomats are explorers of the realities of world politics. They navigate paths of contrasts and ambiguities, heeding Bismarckian choices: "the least harmful, the most useful." Diplomats are among the great adopters in history. Within the span of a century they have progressed from the old diplomacy through a short era of illusions following the First World War, the brutality and collapse of the European system of diplomacy during the interwar period, the confrontation of the Cold War era, and last the beginning of the twenty-first century, when voluntary nongovernmental entities have attempted to change the long-established conventions and norms of diplomacy.

Being close to power has proved to be a double-edged sword. The relationship between diplomatic envoys and sovereigns poses a challenge to moral philosophy that needs to be addressed. Diplomats may conceal facts, remain silent, obey instructions, and display civility and trust in the service of their country and sovereign, but such behavior seldom leads to glory. On the contrary, politicians and heads of state have a long list of grievances against diplomats. They demand loyalty, but tend to ignore or punish their emissaries when expedient.

Challenges have confronted diplomats in all ages, but their preserved domain was never breached and invaded as has occurred in the last generation. Substate and supranational actors, NGOs and advocate associations of all sorts compete with diplomats amid a plethora of ungovernable channels of communication. Indeed, the balance between the social and political, and the "international" has been dislocated. Diplomats also have to cope with the widening gap between formal representation and the fragmented political entity they represent. The expanding emphasis on civil and human rights and other solidarist endeavors, will further complicate the role of professional diplomats as envoys and human beings. It is, however, doubtful whether there is an appropriate substitute for the skilled diplomat—and whether there is a better trader in concessions and a more acute observer and reporter of international circumstances.

The proposition that the diplomat is a courtier of civilization is far from being utopian or far-fetched. There are, of course, diplomats who live a scandalous life, or are even corrupt. But, diplomats who are true to their mission as messengers of trust and accommodation, and have a grasp of the collective good, are, indeed, courtiers of civilization. Deceit and duplicity are only a short-lived ploy, while truthfulness and responsibility are a necessity stemming from the nobility of the diplomat's métier as a custodian of international virtues, and the norms of a functional and civilized international society. While often they are depicted as cynical pragmatists, good diplomats are crusaders for truth. Observing objectively and reporting accurately are among the fundamental virtues of diplomacy. Thus, virtuous diplomatists embody an inherent connection between their ethics and their professional competence.

Diplomacy is anchored in the humanistic tradition; it is a creative and emancipatory profession manifesting noble human faculties that have withstood the test of time. The diplomat is the messenger of an ethically redeeming mission. But, the diplomat's calling as a moral agent has been forfeited, not only by the anarchic nature of international relations, but also by political betrayal and public misunderstanding. Diplomacy has been fragmented, and relegated to a secondary role, losing its potential vitality. Diplomats must not be confined by their formality and exclusiveness, nor operate in an apologetic mood, for diplomacy offers the most reasonable way of conducting relations between political entities.

—— ·•· ——

I wish to record my gratitude to all whom I am indebted throughout the writing of this book. I wish to thank Norman Rose for his magnanimity and unfailing support. The Leonard Davis Institute and the Watson Institute, and James Der Derian in particular, have provided timely support and encouragement. I acknowledge with gratitude the assistance given to me at the Library for Humanities and Social Sciences at the Hebrew University and the Rockefeller Library at Brown University.

I am deeply thankful to Kari Druck, for her kindness and unrivaled expertise, and to Dorothea Shefer-Vanson for editing the manuscript with such a meticulous way. I am very thankful to the two anonymous readers for their constructive and thoughtful comments. I wish to pay tribute to my fellows at the Diplomatic Studies and the English School sections in the International Studies Association for choosing the golden rule—neither succumbing to realist pessimism, nor to solidarist illusions.

Joe and Meredith Powers have generously provided my family with comfortable accommodation while staying in Providence. I should especially like to thank all those at the State University of New York Press who helped in various ways toward publication of this book. Michael Rinella was a courteous and expert editor. Ryan Morris and Anne Valentine have expertly and efficiently taken care of the book's production and its marketing. Laura Glenn has copyedited the book with diligence and expertise. My thanks are extended also to Rafael Chaiken and Emily Keneston.

Last, my profound thanks go to my wife Leah and our children—Hamoutal, Rottem, and Ido.

1

— ⋅•⋅ —

Notes on the Origins and Evolution of the Diplomatic Mission

DIPLOMACY HAS A civilizational standing, and agreed practices common to diverse political entities. It flourishes best in conditions of political fragmentation, where there is a measure of autonomy in the conduct of external affairs, and common norms exist. Diplomacy was founded out of necessity and based on common sense and reciprocity. Watson is right to comment that "We should be impressed by what seems permanent in diplomacy."[1] We find rough similarities in the evolution of diplomacy, namely, the despatch of emissaries of high social standing, provision of immunity to envoys, and the ornamentation of practice with rituals and ceremonies.

Prehistorical diplomacy, sometimes referred to as the anthropological stage in the evolution of diplomacy, is shrouded by speculation, but is also characterized by prodigious optimism. This assumed "state of nature" points to a measure of rational calculation and a desire to cooperate with others. The reverse may, indeed, also be inferred. The decline of diplomacy is an indication of human failure, if not of a civilizational crisis.

In the midst of historical turmoil, or a golden age, the principal actor of diplomacy—the ambassador, envoy, or herald—endures. Their existential predicament never changes as they constantly remain dependent on the ruling class. For a very long time preoccupation with diplomacy required courage, a quality not naturally associated with diplomats. Diplomats were confronted by hazards on various fronts—the whims and vagaries of their sovereigns, the risks encountered during their travels, and the vicissitudes awaiting them in foreign countries. The safety of

1

diplomats, despite all their immunity and privileges, was precarious at best. This continues to be the case.

Diplomacy was neither a feature of all human civilizations nor a preconceived idea. Although, we have no conclusive evidence about the origins of ancient diplomacy, the circumstances of its beginnings were quite harsh. The relations between alien tribes, usually accompanied by rituals and taboos, reveal a recurrent design, that of sending emissaries in periods of war and peace. Diplomatic practices evolved out of necessity, sanctioned by custom and religion and fortified by reciprocity.[2] Magic and religious sanctity augmented the belief that heralds possessed a supernatural power that it would be fatal to violate.[3] It was found both practical and necessary to have emissaries whose lives had to be protected.

Throughout history emissaries were men of high social standing, a fact that facilitated their task of mediation, but did not protect them from the hardships of their occupation. From the very beginning, certain human qualities were associated with the diplomatic character—caution, fair judgment, politeness in facing the more powerful, and the ability to handle delicate social and political situations. In these imagined diplomatic encounters of the past, diplomatic envoys were quite limited in their capacity to influence the basic circumstances of their mission, and they must have relied on a strong feeling of self-identity as well as on an intuitive understanding of the other side.

The immunity that allowed diplomatic missions to be accomplished originated in a universal bond, that of a religious sanction. But the safety of the diplomat, even given the existence of this sanction, could be violated. Diplomats were vulnerable to punishment, imprisonment, or even execution. They were also considered to be strangers who had to undergo ritual purification before being permitted to perform their mission.[4]

The controversy about the origin of diplomacy reached a culminating point with the introduction of the diplomatic tradition of the Ancient Near East. Whether the Amarna and Mari archives constitute evidence of a well-developed diplomatic practice preceded by many centuries, but also leading to the classical period of Greece and Rome, is of less importance for understanding the role of diplomatic practitioners. It seems that they carried out a similar repertoire of actions. Diplomacy, however, throughout all ages and regions, is still assessed, measured, and evaluated by Western standards. This, of course, does not negate the achievements of the ancient Near Eastern kingdoms. Diplomacy is not a strictly Western phenomenon. Evidently, wherever civilization blossomed, diplomacy flourished, though European diplomacy was the most developed and the most influential.

The problem of dating and interpreting historical events and ancient texts is still a formidable one, and the evaluation of the diplomacy of the ancient Near Eastern ranges from one that was sophisticated and efficient to one that was rudimentary and crude.[5] What we know about the diplomats of the ancient Near East is based on about 50 documents (out of 350) dating from the mid-fourteenth century B.C., found at Tel Al-Amarna, Egypt, in 1887. The later discovery of the Royal archive of Mari dating from the first half of the eighteenth century B.C., testifies to the continuity of the same diplomatic tradition.[6] Correspondents with Egypt in the Amarna letters are Mittani, Hatti, Assyria, and Babylonia. The letters were written on clay tablets in cuneiform script. The language of most of the letters is Akkadian, the presumed lingua franca of that period.

A diplomatic envoy of the Mari and the Amarna periods may have been well qualified, and was usually of a high standing in court. He had, first and foremost, to survive the battle of gladiators in conditions of uncertainty and risk. There is no conclusive evidence to indicate that messengers carried a formal document recognized by all parties to safeguard their journey to the country of their mission. Ambassadorial activity was hazardous, and escort troops were frequently needed against attack. Envoys traveled together as a group; their companions could have been soldiers or fellow messengers. Envoys did not escape imprisonment, and the possibility of being kidnapped or even assassinated. Even if the custom of hospitality existed, not every kingdom was in full control of its territory.[7]

The relationship between allied rulers was perceived as one of kinship, fraternity, or subordination, which could affect the attitude toward envoys. Courtesy and respect were reflected in the envoy's reception, escort, and timely dismissal. Permission to leave was at the discretion of the host king, a privilege that allowed for the possibility of exerting pressure on or intimidating the envoy.[8]

It is not clear to what extent envoys were free to fulfill their tasks. They could be invited to important state functions, but envoys of hostile kingdoms could also be kept outside the city gates. In the case of allied powers, envoys were put up in a designated residence, and the host king provided for their daily needs. The envoy's functions may look familiar to us—to report on political conditions, gather information on military affairs, and arrange for the exchange of gifts and royal visits.[9]

There is no evidence for a permanent residence in the ancient Near East. Even when envoys stayed for a long period of time, their appointment was for a specific purpose, conveying strictly the message of their sovereign. Nonetheless, there is evidence of instances, including the important case of a delegation to Hammurabi, the Babylonian king, where it was left to the discretion of the envoys to work out the details of a possible agreement. In the absence of valid norms, however, the rise and fall of the diplomacy of the ancient Near East rested on the exact interpretation of reciprocal acts and impressions understood only by their ad-hoc terms.

—— ••• ——

The diplomatic traditions of the two ancient empires of India and China, which were in a regular contact with other civilizations, are presented almost as a digression in the history of diplomacy. The diplomacy of India flourished in the fourth century B.C. Kautilya, counselor to King Chandragupta, was almost a contemporary of Aristotle, and it would seem that his notorious *Arthashastra* was composed following Alexander's invasion of India.[10] Diplomacy is presented as the inherent art of government, where crafty diplomats labored in contentious fronts among sixteen nations (Mahajanapadas). Envoys, usually appointed for ad-hoc missions, could have full power to negotiate. The rank of an ambassador (*duta*) was given to a select few, and those who were closest to the king.[11] The stratagems of Indian diplomacy were judged by the results they produced, where the best guarantee for a treaty was the king's good faith.

Indian envoys appear to have been accorded the broadest repertoire possible. It could have ranged from the clandestine and treacherous, to the *dharma*, the moral code of righteousness and duty.[12] Indian diplomacy tended toward realpolitik. Beyond maintaining alliances, gathering information, and transmitting the views of kings, envoys were required to threaten, appease, or exert pressure, sow dissention, incite a revolt against a warring king, and be a divisive force in court.

Indian emissaries were instructed to prepare themselves, mentally and physically, for their mission, and reflect on their likely diplomatic presentation and maneuvers. An envoy has to be precise in the delivery of his message, regardless of the reaction to its content. He was immune, in principle, as he was merely repeating the words of his master, but he had to be on his guard against various dangers and be prepared to escape. Indeed, he was required to be permanently cautious, avoid women and drink, and sleep alone. Being subject to clandestine practices and the violation of the law, the envoy's precarious situation was inherent in Indian diplomacy.

Chinese ancient diplomacy was a secluded and self-creating domain. The Empire was regarded as the center of the world, the rest being left to the Barbarian quarters. It was an ethnocentric dichotomy that has impeded the integration of China into international politics.

Chinese diplomacy flourished when the country was not unified, between the eighth and the third centuries B.C.[13] The Chinese emissary had to accommodate himself into a tight and ritualistic world, full of violence and mistrust, where his safety was precarious and his obedience to the emperor was absolute. It seems also, that his social status was quite low. The plight of a foreign envoy was even worse. Barbarians were ranked as no more than unequal vassals, and had to go through the humiliating Kowtow ceremony.

Despite imperial whims and restriction, Chinese envoys played an essential role as emissaries between warring Chinese states, conveying their masters' orders, but doing so on a temporary basis and with no permanent residency.

— .•. —

Ancient Greece was the battleground of internal stasis and rivalry for hegemony. However, the Greeks shared a common culture that allowed diplomacy to be conducted among equals, albeit with a manifest ethnocentric identity. Greek diplomacy was conducted publicly, and internal dissentions and inflammatory rhetoric were an integral part of its repertoire, while alliances and external commitments were not always abiding. Pan-Hellenic institutions and religious festivities played a restrictive role, and constituted a forum for consultation.[14] By most accounts, Greek diplomacy is not considered to be highly developed, particularly, in the formal aspects of the diplomatic practice. The institution of the *proxenia* should be evaluated differently. The *proxenos* may be regarded as playing one of the most innovative roles in the evolution of diplomacy.

Diplomatic emissaries in ancient Greece are denoted by a variety of terms—*kerykes* (heralds), *presbeis* (envoys), and *angeloi* (messengers). None of the three ranks was concerned only with diplomacy.[15] The *kerykes*, the designated descendents of the wily and mischievous Hermes, were the most established in Greek tradition and their status was sanctified by religious ceremonies. The *kerykes* were the closest to having a diplomatic immunity, but there is evidence that Greek envoys were arrested, and in rare cases, even murdered.

Kerykes were men of high standing chosen also for their eloquence and force of persuasion, which was essential. The presentation of a case before a city-state assembly is magnificently described by Thucydides, who placed the Greek emissary between the Scylla of the assembly's temperament and the Charybdis of his own rhetorical skills.[16]

Greek embassies usually consisted of between three and ten members, and were of short duration. Traditionally they were hosted by their *proxenos* or stayed at an inn. The mission of envoys was closely scrutinized by the *polis* authority, particularly in the case of Athens, and usually had simple instructions. They presented and concluded what had been already decided on by assemblies and councils. Thus, envoys were left with little flexibility in their deliberations, and were either rewarded modestly for their diplomatic achievement or penalized in the case of a failure. They were also obliged to submit an expense account. Nonetheless, public distinction was reward enough, and a valued prize for those who were also politicians. Diplomatic missions were very politicized, and could result in fierce disputes. A notable case was the Athenian embassy to the Macedonian court, which included Demosthenes and his rival Aeschines.[17]

The institution of *proxenia* was a Hellenistic invention made possible by the cultural affinity among the Greeks. The role of the *proxenos*, the representative of a different *polis* than his native one, was extremely complicated. The *proxenia* was an appointment reserved for leading political figures, but it could be obtained as a family inheritance, thus making it a diplomatic role with a certain permanency.[18]

With no official standing in his *polis*, and serving as a host to foreign envoys, the loyalty of the *proxenos* became questionable. Particularly in turbulent times, which involved fierce factional struggles, the *proxenos* was vulnerable to attacks or suspected of being a potential fifth columnist.[19] This delicate position required the *proxenos* to possess extraordinary diplomatic and oratorical skills. This was, indeed, the case with the *proxenoi* of fame—the Athenians Demosthenes, Nicias, and Alcibiades, and the Theban poet Pindar. The *proxenia* brought mixed blessings; it involved fame and influence, but it was incriminatory and bore no direct financial rewards.

— ••• —

Historians of diplomacy tend to underestimate the achievements of Roman diplomacy. Nicolson claims that the Romans failed owing to their "political masterfulness," and Campbell refers to an "unstructured and unsystematic" conduct of diplomacy.[20] It is true that Roman diplomacy was that of the hegemon. But it was also based on Roman dignity and good faith (*Fides Romana*), and a belief in the legal sanctity of contracts. Military dominance was balanced by senatorial political subtlety, and occasionally by the diplomatic pragmatism of proconsuls in the provinces.

The Roman legal tradition laid the foundation for well-defined and applicable international concepts and ideas. The *ius gentium* and the *ius naturalis* were of immense influence on Western political thought, particularly on the laws of war and peace and the universality of international laws. The rules of *pacta servanda sunt, amicitia, foedus, and societas* are still with us.

Roman diplomacy during the era of the Republic was conducted by *legates*, observed formally by the *fetiales* and controlled by the Senate. The *fetiales*, a priestly college, presided over diplomatic rituals and ceremonies, kept diplomatic records and interpreted them if needed. The *fetailes* had lost the importance bestowed on them in the early days of the Republic, though they sometimes accompanied *legates*, as was the case with Scipio's delegation to Carthage.[21] Roman *legates* (also *nuntii* or *orators*) were appointed by the Senate from among the patricians, who were supposed to act in accordance with Roman virtues. Acting on an ad hoc basis, *legates* had relative *auctoritas* for diplomatic initiative, however, on returning they reported to the Senate, the ultimate authority in foreign affairs.

In principle, Rome preserved the immunity of diplomatic envoys, but the universality of this practice is questionable. Roman delegations were escorted by a substantial force, particularly in times of war.[22] The *ius gentium* provided qualified immunity for foreign envoys, but they had to go through a humiliating reception until they were heard by the Senate.[23] When envoys were viewed unfavorably, they were relegated to the status of *speculatores* (spies) and escorted from Rome under armed guard.

— ᵔᵔ —

Medieval Byzantium was the discontinuous replica of Western Europe. Erected, presumably, on similar pillars—Roman tradition, classical culture and Christianity—it faced an utterly different historical fate. For all its splendor and intricacies, and the outstanding ability of its diplomats to bridge the gap between appearances and reality, Byzantium survived precariously for over a millennium (ca. 330–1453). Byzantium was a Christian realm surrounded by many enemies with different beliefs and substantial military power—Persians, Huns, Arabs, Goths, Bulgars, Hungarians, Pechanges, and eventually Turks, who destroyed the Empire. The Byzantine *Oikoumene*, whose imagined borders included the entire civilized world and whose inhabitants professed Orthodox Christianity, inherited the insecurities of the *Limes Romanus*. In reality, its influence extended to the eastern Mediterranean, the Middle East, Russia, and Italy, and ultimately exerted enduring influence by merging the diplomatic traditions of West and East that were adopted by the city-states of Italy.[24]

Facing enemies on two fronts and aware of the limited resources of the Empire, Byzantine diplomacy was imaginative and defensive, but not passive. It acquired a justifiable reputation for treachery and deception, but Byzantine diplomats were masters of their craft. Byzantine diplomatic protocol displayed the supremacy of the Empire, manipulating the dual images of Constantinople as the Second Rome, and the notion that the Emperor was the divinely appointed father of all men. Byzantine diplomats adhered to the strategy of the indirect approach, incorporating delays with avoidance of the unnecessary resort to force. To that end, they employed elaborate methods of gathering information, which was supplied to embassies, and enabled a flexible and prompt response to new developments. In addition, the Byzantine system of bribery bought allegiance and submission by granting honorific titles, and making calculated and timely marriages.[25]

Byzantium was, perhaps, the first to institutionalize the training of diplomatic envoys. The Emperor directed the Empire's diplomacy with the assistance of a relatively small number of officials. Byzantine diplomats, recruited and carefully trained, employed their diplomatic functions to the full in order to propagate the grandeur and invincibility of the Empire. They were instructed to gather information, report on the strength and weakness of tribes and Barbarian courts, negotiate, but also to honor local customs and manners. In this case, linguistic competence was of the utmost importance. The conduct of diplomacy was assumed to be coordinated with the various fiscal, ecclesiastical and military agencies.[26]

Byzantine diplomacy reached its apex of rituals and ceremonies in an attempt to solidify the Emperor's projection of wealth, strength, and benevolent virtues. Byzantium inherited the Roman tradition in its attitude to foreign envoys. They were accommodated in a special residence, and kept under constant surveillance that amounted to virtual captivity. Envoys were escorted by a special staff of *scrinium Barbarorum* (the office of the Barbarians), which was directed by the *logothete* who was also responsible for the supervision of the imperial diplomatic envoys.[27]

— •◦• —

Historians of the Middle Ages agree that at that time diplomacy was in decline and notoriously inconsistent, and that without Venice the continuity of diplomacy would have been disrupted.[28] Notwithstanding this criticism, certain considerations should be taken into account. European society had to adapt itself to harsh material circumstances, and to appalling means of communication. Latin Christendom regarded itself to be one *Respublica Christiana*, but the complicated feudal system allowed principals, provinces, cities, and the Church, but also noblemen and *condottieri*, to send out emissaries and take part in a diversified network of diplomacy. Obviously, diplomatic practice was not clear cut. As a matter of fact, there was no defined *droit d'ambassade* until the end of the sixteenth century.[29]

During the Middle Ages envoys struggled with the perilous environment, being a target for robbery, and the abuse of their privileges. Resistance to undertaking diplomatic mission is understandable, because of the sacrifice in time and money and the hazards of travel. A considerable lapse of time occurred between the decision to send an envoy and his departure, largely owing to such circumstances.[30] Princes and noblemen became the main protectors of their emissaries, providing them with letters of safe conduct and letters of introduction. If necessary, they resorted to the practice of taking hostages during envoys' missions, threatening reprisals to anyone injuring their own emissaries. The Papal *nuntius* was also safeguarded by the *privilagium clericale*, which exempted him from the King's criminal jurisdiction.[31] But diplomats remained vulnerable, and a measure of courage was a prerequisite for undertaking a diplomatic mission.

An envoy was known as a *Legatus*, and sometimes a *nuntius* or *missus*, and was usually chosen from among the nobility or clergymen. By the late Middle Ages a distinction had been made between three diplomatic classes—the *nuntius*, the *procurator*, and the ambassador or orator. According to Bernard de Rosier, the provost of Toulouse, who summed up the ambassadorial practice of the Middle Ages toward the beginning of the fifteenth century, it is apparent that the term *ambassador* was in use in Italy as early as in the thirteenth century.[32] The revival of Roman law brought back the term *procurator*, a legal representative with ad hoc *plena potentas* to negotiate. It was a role that was not completely defined, and allowed room for maneuvering, though it carried the risk that any failure would be attributed to the *procurator* personally.[33] The rising conception of personal representation, where the diplomat personified his sovereign, opened the door for precedence quarrels that were to haunt European diplomacy until the end of the eighteenth century.

By the mid-fourteenth century a distinction between *ambaxador* and regular envoys had been introduced in Venice. The Papacy called envoys who were not cardinals *legates*, or *nuntius*, as is the case to this day.[34] Diplomacy flourished under the authority of the Church already in the eleventh century. The clergy constituted an abundant source of expert diplomatic emissaries for the Papacy, and were in the service of all the other principals.

— ••• —

Under the influence of Byzantium, the Republic of Venice had an extensive impact on the diplomatic patterns adopted by the city-states of Italy, and the rest of Europe. The Venetian *Relazioni* preserved for posterity the history of a unique and refined diplomatic system. The Venetian practice of registering all diplomatic transactions is quite exemplary; not only regular diplomatic dispatches were recorded, but also a full account of Venetian missions (883–1797) and the deliberations of the political body concerning their envoys.[35]

Venice exemplifies a notorious case of a tightly controlled diplomatic system, with all its benefits and disadvantages. Indeed, a considerable part of Venetian legislation was concerned with ambassadors, and the attempt to limit the expenses of diplomatic missions. Nonetheless, Venetian diplomacy was impressive in many ways, and its practitioners were admired for their high standards and their devotion to the Republic.[36]

The diplomatic service of Venice, as appropriate to a society immersed in the life of commerce, developed an admirable talent for collecting information based on well-situated posts across the Mediterranean and the Levant. According to Ermolao Barbaro in the *De Officio Legati*, the Venetian diplomats served their city-state, "to advise and think whatever may best serve the preservation and aggrandizement" of Venice.[37] Diplomatic missions were entrusted to officers who were selected with the utmost care, usually from among educated and talented noblemen. During his mission, a Venetian envoy was governed by rigorous measures. He was denied the company of his wife, was instructed not to share his opinion beyond governmental circles, and denied the privilege of receiving gifts from a foreign sovereign. Under this austere style of life, with its modest financial reward against heavy expenses, Venetian citizens were reluctant to be diplomats. The difficulty of filling ambassadorial offices became a serious impediment that necessitated the imposition of penalties on noblemen who declined to serve as ambassadors.[38]

Venetian ambassadors labored under the strict and careful instruction of the state. They were also advised by the dispatches of other diplomatic envoys, and by newsletters (*Avvisi*) that kept them in touch with Venetian affairs. Their first task on returning was to provide a comprehensive account of their mission, which was submitted to the College of the *Signory* and the Senate.

— •◦• —

The resident embassy, the master institution of diplomacy, in the words of Martin Wight, was by all accounts a Western innovation.[39] From the late Renaissance the diplomatic mission flourished under European hegemony. The main stages in this development were the disintegration of Medieval Christendom, the rise of the sovereign state, and the beginning of European international society.

Residential embassies emerged among the Italian city-states between the Peace of Lodi (1454) and the end of the fifteenth century, and hence the practice was adopted by states north of Italy. There is no agreement as to the exact date of the first permanent embassy, but this is, perhaps, an obsession with origins. Nicodemo da Pontremoli, the resident ambassador of Milan at Florence for seventeen years (1450–1467), is frequently considered to have been the first resident ambassador. Although it is evident that envoys under Francesco Sforza, the Duke of Milan, were active in this period, resident embassies may have begun earlier. But Mattingly writes that as a result of the length and the distinction of his mission, Nicodemo deserves to be remembered as the first resident ambassador.[40]

The beginning of resident embassies was a defining moment in the history of diplomacy. Diplomatic practice acquired new possibilities and the ambassadorial horizon was dramatically expanded. The ambassador was now in the best position to gather information, represent his sovereign, and study the intentions of other countries. The refinement of the diplomatic mission resulted in a significant increase in the ambassadorial workload. The beginning of residence also ushered in an obsession with secrecy and the fear of spying. The moral duty of the ambassador and his loyalty acquired new significance.[41]

In the two centuries between the Peace of Lodi and the Peace of Westphalia, the ways and means of diplomacy gradually changed. Collective embassies, with ambassadors of equal ranks, and "circular" ones, ceased to exist. Taking oaths to observe a treaty, or taking hostages to guarantee its observance, gradually disappeared. After surviving the religious wars of the seventeenth century, diplomacy became hierarchical and more secretive. It was France under the Bourbons that emerged with the largest number of expert ambassadors, with French becoming the *lingua franca* of diplomacy. Matters of precedence and prestige marred relations among the European sovereigns, and only in 1815 was the diplomatic hierarchy established with the Vienna Règlement. But the aristocratic composition of diplomacy lasted until the First World War.[42]

2

——— ·◆· ———

Voices for Diplomacy

Statesmen, Diplomats, and Philosophers

D IPLOMACY EVOLVED less as a product of the human imagination than by the way it was practiced. Despite broad agreement on many aspects of diplomacy, versions of its definition and description abound. While routines, procedures, and settings have been modified or abolished altogether, the nature of diplomacy has an enduring validity. Historians of the remote past, as well as contemporary scholars, ask the same question: Why and in what way did human relations come to be regarded as a matter for diplomacy? We may ask also whether there is any correspondence between the essence of diplomacy as it is understood by scholars and philosophers and the way it is practiced by professional diplomats.

There is a certain dialectic in the attempt to define diplomacy. In its inclusive definition diplomacy has come a full circle. The attempt at present is to include relations of various sorts as legitimate diplomatic activity, and thus depriving the state of its centrality. A reversal of diplomacy to its early phases is now bound together with vast technological advances.[1] Will the achievement of political philosophers, lawyers, and diplomatists in establishing diplomacy as the foremost method of conducting relations between sovereign states survive the contemporary onslaught? Evidently, the Westphalian order, for some theorists a "straitjacket" that blocked the emancipation of international affairs, enabled an international European society to flourish, ultimately becoming a universal one.

A second necessary precaution in evaluating the essence of diplomacy is the tendency to define it as an art, and as such as largely the domain of the virtuous statesman. That is a tradition that a priori diminishes the role of the professional diplomat, and in some cases deprives diplomacy of its ethical foundations.

Definitions of diplomacy emphasize either its practice or its virtues as a civilized dialogue and a moderating method. Indeed, diplomacy is a unique human encounter, the result of conflict or estrangement between nations or social groups.[2] As long as the state remains at the center of international relations, diplomacy will be anchored in the political domain, aspiring to relations without resorting to force. There is no adequate alternative for diplomatic practice as the most prudent method for reconciling contradictory interests, or for other parties to agree to an accepted resolution.

There is an inherent and inevitable rationality in diplomacy as a peaceful and consent-based method. "It seems," Nicolson writes, "by the use of reason, conciliation and the exchange of interests, to prevent major conflicts arising between sovereign states."[3] Diplomacy's constructive task is to secure order and stability under changing circumstances. Richelieu, who adhered to the concept of "continuous negotiation," established a correlation between the national interest and the collective good by securing an international equilibrium that served all states. It was, at least until the rise of modern dictatorships, the moral obligation of the great powers to preserve the world order. This is the only way to consider the diplomacy of Metternich, Bismarck, and Kissinger as a benevolent act.

The essence of diplomacy should also be sought in the preserved domain of its professional practitioners, the fully fledged practice of diplomats, an activity refined by training and experience and subject to "tact and intelligence." No doubt, diplomats tend to stress the distance between theory and experience. Abba Eban sums up the diplomat's point of view: "diplomacy has to be empirical, pragmatic and intuitive . . . it depends, in the last resort, on the way in which its practitioners react to opportunities and dangers as they arise."[4] And last, we may trace the nature of diplomacy in its idealistic portrayal as an international collective good, a redeeming method in the enduring progress toward the *Civitas Maxima.*[5]

—— ·•· ——

Four approaches should be considered in the attempt to define the essence of diplomacy. The first is the realist school from Commynes and Machiavelli to Wicquefort; the second is the integrative-prudent approach of Callières, Satow, and Nicolson; the third ranges from Guicciardini and Gentili to Grotius, Vattel, and the English School, which accords primacy to law, cultural aspects, and political thought in an established international society; and last, the contemporary inclusive approach regards diplomacy as a human discourse emanating from estrangement or sameness, performed in changing places and forms, and conducted by various personalities, not necessarily professional diplomats.

In Machiavelli's (1469–1527) grammar of power the diplomat is secondary to the Captain of War. Apparently, Machiavelli displays less originality in his writing on diplomacy as is evinced by his "advice to Raffaello Girolami."[6] The diplomat, however, plays an important auxiliary role for his prince's benefit. As military strength and constant readiness are vital to the safety of the state, the gathering of information, the study of intentions and exact reporting become essential functions of the diplomat. Diplomacy supports the sovereign's virtue. Machiavelli advises the ambassador to be on guard, as "good policy, whoever suggests it, comes from the wisdom of the prince."[7]

In contrast to Machiavelli, the ambassador is portrayed by Cummynes (ca. 1447–1511) as a virtuous actor. Proclaiming his distaste for summitry, Cummynes asserts that the ambassador's duty is to minimize the number of encounters between sovereigns. Cummynes raises, of course, one of the arguments most favored by diplomas. He is, on the other hand, utterly counterproductive in his other advice. Foreign ambassadors are to be honorably received, but should be mistrusted and dispatched back as soon as possible.[8]

Richelieu (1585–1642), chief minister to King Louis XIII, was the architect of the alliance between France and Sweden that decided the fate of the Habsburgs in the Thirty Years War, paving the way for Louis XIV's absolutism and the invention of the French system of diplomacy.[9] In Richelieu's construct of "continuous negotiation" diplomacy was integrated as a permanent part of the raison d'état. Diplomats should pursue national ends, though not necessarily in contradiction to the interests of other states that are members of the same balance of power. Richelieu's success in centralizing the diplomatic machinery, expanded the diplomats' repertoire of action, and their ability to exploit the right moment: "he who negotiates continuously will finally find the right instant to attain his ends."[10] Richelieu enhanced the reputation of the professional diplomat, maintaining that he should be a master of his craft, intelligent and politically ethical, regarding keeping promises as the most reasonable and prudent way of conducting diplomacy.[11]

It was left to Lipsius and Wicquefort, both from the Netherlands, to augment Machiavelli's realism with a prudent approach to the practice of diplomacy. Both of their manuals became most influential in the seventeenth century. Justus Lipsius (1547–1606), a disciple of Tacitus, a

Latin scholar, and Stoic in inclination, praised virtue and prudence as the major guidelines for action, and thus for the practice of diplomacy. He claimed that moderation, discipline, and adhering to promises and the law were conducive to diplomatic success. Lipsius nonetheless distinguished between personal morality and the need to depart from it, if necessary, in the public domain.[12]

Abraham de Wicquefort's crafty and far more detailed manual dwells on the public duties of the diplomat, and the instructions that make him an efficient and prudent practitioner. In his treatise, Wicquefort keeps a distance from a juristic perspective and the laudatory portrayal of the ideal diplomat. Accomplishment is preferable to personal virtues. To be true to his mission, the professional envoy must pursue his main tasks of representation and reporting in a knowledgeable and precise way. Wicquefort establishes the foundations of diplomacy on the law of nations as a symbol of sovereignty. The need for the resident ambassador is the result of the nature of international affairs, not the whims of princes.[13]

Callières, Satow, and Nicolson, all three practicing diplomats, have written integrative treatises on diplomacy. All three were men of letters with solid roots in history, political thought, and literature. Like his British followers, Callières attempted to establish diplomacy as a distinct and autonomous vocation, an integral part of the state's foreign policy, also serving humanity's collective good by its moderating influence. All three considered diplomacy to be the most prudent and civilized way of conducting foreign affairs. As men of the world, they were disillusioned by the realities of politics. Their "enlightened scepticism" led them to regard the use of force as only the last resort, and to detest dogmatism in all its disguises. Lastly, Callières, Satow, and Nicolson praised honesty as the best way of conducting diplomacy.[14]

François de Callières (1645–1717) published his much acclaimed *De la manière de négocier avec les souverains* following the death of Louis XIV, when France was losing its dominance, and Europe was becoming an international society. The scene was set for defining diplomacy in a prudent and civilized manner, and for paying attention to the professional aspects of diplomacy, and in particular the training and schooling of diplomats. Callières himself was an admirable representative of the French system—its excellence in negotiation and clarity of expression.[15] While Callières was of the opinion that there were occasions when a diplomat was obliged to be an "honorable spy," his portrayal of the diplomat does not make it necessary for him to be one. The diplomat searches for accommodation through "the force of reason and persuasion," and in accordance with the principles and rules of the law of nations. Callières's diplomat is a civil servant, and a knowledgeable and honest courtier. Diplomacy is a definable profession. Thus, the talents and virtues required of its practitioner are not necessarily those of the nobility or of military men.[16] He was, indeed, decisive in his preference for the professional diplomat: "a small number of ministers, well chosen and disposed in several states of Europe, are capable of rendering to the prince, or state which employs them very great services: who with a small expense do frequently as much service as standing armies."[17]

Ernest Satow (1843–1929), an outstanding diplomat of his time, has written, perhaps, the most scholarly and comprehensive guide to diplomatic practices.[18] His definition of diplomacy as "the application of intelligence and tact," often brushed aside as self-evident, fully reflects his understanding of diplomacy as the civilized pursuit of state interests.[19] Diplomacy, after all, is a constant search for complementary interests, and its moderating influence is first and foremost the responsibility of the great powers. Satow's portrait of the diplomat is that of a honorable representative of his country with manifest talents and virtues: "prudence, foresight, intelligence, penetration, wisdom."[20] And like Nicolson he was a traditionalist in his criticism of summitry and open diplomacy.

Harold Nicolson (1886–1968), a diplomat and a man of letters, was also a penetrating observer of international history. His *Diplomacy* remains the most popular book of its kind in the twentieth century. Nicolson viewed the old school of diplomacy as the only ordered way of conducting relations between rival states, and was bewildered by the weakening of the European diplomatic tradition and the populist bend of open diplomacy.[21] Democratic diplomacy, which had already been criticized by Tocqueville, seemed to him to introduce alien elements that distanced it from the virtues of precision, moderation, and tolerance.

President Wilson's performance at Versailles, and international history between the two world wars, augmented his mistrust of politicians as amateur and populist. Nicolson, nonetheless, emphatically distinguished diplomacy from foreign policy. Diplomacy is "not a purpose but a method."[22] Even when the contribution of diplomats to foreign policy is of importance, they still need political guidance in order to adjust their endeavors to the principles and aims of their governments. Though relating to diplomacy as the most protean of all branches of human activity, Nicolson saw no other guarantor of peaceful relations among nations.[23]

— •◆• —

In the early modern period, diplomats, lawyers and political philosophers introduced a more consensual understanding of diplomacy. The *Ricordi* of Francesco Guicciardini (1483–1540), presents diplomacy in a rather pragmatic and tolerant way. A contemporary of Machiavelli, Guicciardini had a distinguished career as an ambassador to Spain and as governor of several Italian city-states. As a man of action, he viewed diplomacy as an essential tool in preserving the balance of power in a measured way. Guicciardini also paid attention to the delicate relations between the diplomatic envoy and his sovereign regarding their cooperation as being imperative for political success.[24]

Alberico Gentili (1552–1608), a Regius Professor of civil law at Oxford University, defined diplomatic law as a coherent whole. His treatise *De Legationibus Libri Tres*, established the immunity and rights of ambassadors as the vital prerequisite for the practice of diplomacy. While displaying ambivalence regarding resident embassies, he emphasized tact and prudence in his portrayal of the best ambassador.[25]

Hugo Grotius (1583–1645), in his *De jure belli ac pacis*, and Emmerich de Vattel (1714–1767) in *Le Droit des Gens*, refined diplomacy's role in the grand design of international society. Grotius, a classicist, lawyer, Latin historian and for a while ambassador for Sweden in Paris, advanced the law of nations as the source of the right for legation, and the exclusive attribute of sovereignty. The foundations of the Roman law of nature (*ius naturalis*) are manifest in Grotius's benevolent view of human nature, and his trust in rationality. Diplomacy is introduced as an institution through which the values and interests of international society can be defended and advanced. Well before the Peace of Westphalia, Grotius was an advocate of Europe as a single international commonwealth, in which great powers, bound by the same rules and norms, preserve peace and stability.[26] A century after Grotius, Vattel described the states of Europe as a single body, bound by a common effort to safeguard the welfare and safety of nations. International relations were to be conducted in terms of perfect equality between states. Vattel preserved Grotius's pluralism, and the balance between the sovereign rights of the state and its membership of international society.[27] It is, perhaps, ironic that Vattel was in agreement with Commynes in his attitude to summitry. Relations between states were to be conducted by "public Ministers."

— .•. —

The English School is the only theoretical approach that places diplomacy as a central concept in its pluralist idea of international society. Indeed, scholars of the English School have provided the richest account of writing on diplomacy. Neither ignoring power politics, nor advocating a preponderance of morality, diplomacy becomes an integral part of the humanistic tradition. At its best, argued Martin Wight, diplomacy embodies honesty, moderation, a sense of proportion and respect for the other side.[28] Diplomacy acquires its fullest meaning as an institution of international society of equal and sovereign states, where its main function is to "circumvent the occasions of war."[29] Lurking above this pragmatic and morally reasonable view is Burke's "empire of circumstances," with all the diversity and complexity of relations among sovereign states.

The current inclusive approach attempts to define diplomacy as being embedded in social relationships, which are occasionally ordered even without the state. It also constructs a discourse that is centered on the individual in a presumed "homo-diplomacy."[30] As a matter of fact, Ada Bozeman was the first to claim that ". . . diplomacy is not a socially autonomous institution, but an outgrowth of the society in which it is practiced."[31]

The inclusive approach may extend the horizon of diplomacy, but results in fragmentation into individuals and groups with diverse, not necessarily political aims. The diminishing status of the diplomat as the legitimate envoy of his country, is hardly an emancipatory alternative to the existing system. It is too early to judge whether the new discourse on diplomacy will be able to offer a meaningful and viable reform to diplomatic practice.[32] Past attempts to deviate from the recognized nature of diplomacy have always failed.

— •◆• —

What do diplomats, as well as statesmen, make of all the talents and virtues that are attributed to them in the vast literature on diplomacy? Statecraft is not an intellectual endeavor, and statesmen of fame, such as Metternich and Kissinger, who regard diplomacy as an art, relegate diplomats to a secondary role, if at all. The virtuous statesman of the past aspired for order, a balanced achievement, rather than a triumph, recognizing that there is no absolute security, or ultimate solution. One has to seize the moment, take domestic constraints into consideration, and be aware of the fundamental tension between power and morality.[33]

It is no mere accident that historians and commentators on diplomacy view the Congress of Vienna and the Concert of Europe with such interest and a sense of vindication. The meeting between Metternich and Bonaparte in Dresden on June 26, 1813, is presented as the triumph of persuasion and calm over power and impatience. Nothing is comparable with Kissinger's praise of Metternich, who, by subtle maneuver, flexibility of tactics, and an extraordinary ability to grasp the fundamentals of the situation, constructed what Gordon Craig described as the most successful modern system of international order.[34]

Kissinger regarded Talleyrand as displaying the greatest similarity to Metternich. A master of his craft, a survivor of three regimes, versatile, and corrupt, Talleyrand secured France's place as an equal partner among the great powers of Europe. Nicolson admired his sense of proportion and ability to seize the moment. By that, Nicolson argues, Talleyrand transcended opportunism to a matter of genius.[35]

Both Nicolson and Kissinger reserve their sharpest criticism for President Woodrow Wilson, regarding his presence in Paris as a cardinal mistake. Nicolson criticizes Wilson for his un-business-like method of negotiation and lack of program, and for his profound but misplaced convictions. Kissinger considers Wilson's statecraft to be the embodiment of the inherent vulnerability of American diplomacy. Wilson's moralism replaced geopolitical judgment. Kissinger preferred and praised Theodore Roosevelt.[36]

Metternich and Bismarck were both ambassadors before their rise to power. Bismarck's case is, perhaps, the most remarkable one of a practitioner who was given the opportunity to direct his nation's foreign policy. Bismarck's memoirs reveal his profound understanding of diplomacy, and its possible entanglement with the ways and means of internal politics.[37] Bismarck's statesmanship reveals his intuitive grasp of reality, precise assessment of rivals, and a search for an acceptable alternative to either war or rivalry. Bismarck confidently remarked that "international policy is a fluid element" that forces the historical actor to choose "the least harmful, the most useful" policy. Kissinger reflects on Bismarck's diplomacy with some compassion. He admires his sense of proportion, tactical flexibility and moderation, and in particular, his understanding of an international equilibrium not as a harmony, but as balance of forces in flux, always leaving room for the unenforceable.[38]

We may make sense A. J. P. Taylor's observation that Bismarck was deceptive in personality, but not in his statesmanship. Ethical and professional observance induced him to call back an influential diplomat from Italy, who reported on meetings in which he did not take part. The ambassador was close to the Kaiser, but was called back nonetheless. Bismarck had chosen well: "between my conviction of the interest of the state and my personal affection for the King."[39] Bismarck expressed with clarity his expectations from the professional diplomat. The diplomat's task, first and foremost, is to foster and improve the external relations of his country, to shun false witticism and court gossip, to concentrate on his tasks, reporting in particular, and to leave to his masters the decision on important matters.[40]

Henry Kissinger dedicates his monumental book on diplomacy to the men and women of the American foreign service. Taking into consideration Kissinger's ambivalence toward the State Department, and professional diplomats in general, one cannot escape the irony. Complains were evident during his active career, compliments were postponed to his retirement.[41]

Kissinger defined diplomacy at the beginning of *A World Restored* as the "art of restraining the exercise of power."[42] In principle, Kissinger adheres to the Machiavellian premise that necessity dictates the statesman's actions, according to the inevitabilities that international reality imposes. There are no absolute values in Kissinger's conception of diplomacy. Balances change according to circumstances, and peace could only be moderate.[43] Even morality is a matter of proportion—neither naked opportunism, nor ethics with no foundation in reality. Kissinger's understanding of diplomacy is instrumental, but prudent. The diplomat assumes his customary role, in assisting the grand moves of the statesmen. It is a dichotomy between policy and bureaucracy, between human grandeur and parochial timidity.[44]

— •◆• —

The vast literature on the ideal diplomat is ridiculed, and not just once, as "vacuous recommendations." Within a span of seventy-five years (1626–1700), 176 treatises on the ideal diplomat were published in Europe. Headly Bull argues that the praiseful recommendations fail to tell us under what conditions diplomatists should possess these virtues, and what object they serve.[45] One may speculate that this laudatory literature was a mirror image of the dubious reputation of the diplomatic envoy, following the establishment of resident embassies in the capitals of Europe. In contrast to the virtues, most suitable to only the most pious and skillful courtiers, Wicquefort wisely comments that they "extend themselves on qualities that are neither proper nor peculiar to him, but without which it is impossible to be either a good citizen or an honest man. . . ."[46]

Despite the tendency to consider the portrait of the ideal diplomat as dated, or perhaps utopian, there are virtues and qualifications of endurable value. Mattingly observes that what Rosier has to say might have been said by modern writers; Anderson writes that inevitably most characteristics of the successful diplomat have not changed over the centuries.[47] Indeed, even if the portrait of the best diplomat is only a fiction, it is worth studying, as it reveals the way diplomacy is comprehended and aspired to.

There are four categories to be examined in the profile of the best diplomat. The first results from his being a civil servant, and accordingly follows a routine where he is both privileged and constrained. The second relates to the skills necessary for performing well within the diplomatic practice. These skills could be acquired, in principle, by training and learning. The third category is a delicate one, as it includes elements that evaluate the diplomat according to his explicit achievement. Diplomatic success, however, is usually concealed and often obscured. The ultimate verdict is to be found in the relations between the diplomat and his government. Tasso remarks rightly that "to have a perfect ambassador you must first have the perfect prince."[48] The last category relates to virtues that are substantial as much as they are subjective. Moral values, beliefs, and convictions are not subject to instruction and training.[49]

The profile of the best diplomat attests to a combination of characteristics that are repeated in most treatises. He must be intelligent, well tempered, persuasive, experienced, have fair judgment, be prudent, and in constant search of accommodation. Cardinal attention is given to the diplomat's moral values, as there is no substitute for integrity and trust.[50]

Callières provides a measured and qualified description of the ideal diplomat. Satow and Nicolson follow the same path. Callières was of the opinion that men are endowed with different talents, but much may be gained by training, experience, and a knowledge of history. The ideal diplomat is a man of reason and prudence, has a good command of himself, and is endowed with an accurate grasp of reality. In addition, gentlemanly manners and political intelligence are important tools for diplomatic representation.[51]

Callières believed that moral and physical courage was a necessary quality for a diplomat who wished to accomplish "any great designs." Apart from a digression about the "honourable spy," Callières regarded honesty as a cardinal virtue, at the same time warning against dogma, abstract contemplation, or qualities destructive to the conduct of diplomacy: "we must not form to ourselves ideas of Plato's Republic in the choice of persons who are designed for these kinds of employment."[52] Callières's advice appears in stronger terms in Nicolson's writings. He regarded missionaries, fanatics, and lawyers as the worst kind of diplomatists.[53]

Satow and Nicolson followed Callières in presenting the ideal diplomat as a man of gentlemanly qualities, with a subtle and perceptive mind, but with human skepticism. Satow praised "diplomatic intelligence," morality, foresight, and experience.[54] Nicolson regarded intelligence and character as equally important, but considered moral integrity as the most important quality for a diplomatist, the second being precision. Relying on Talleyrand and Jules Cambon, he added the importance of calm, patience, and perseverance. In a lecture delivered at the Foreign Office in November 1945, Nicolson defined "reliability" as the most desired quality. In this case, reliability included five components: truthfulness, precision, loyalty, modesty, and a sense of proportion.[55]

3

— •◦• —

Conventions and Rituals

DIPLOMATIC CONVENTIONS and rituals are often described as unnecessary relics of the past; as petty details and formalities anchored in a conservative tradition barely influenced by the changing international reality; and for the most part devoid of substance. Wicquefort, a keen observer and a canny pragmatist, already complained of the tendency to pay attention to matters of representation and ceremony rather than to diplomatic bargains.[1]

It is fair to ask why diplomatic protocol and rituals persisted for so long, and were not replaced by new methods. The answer seems to be quite clear. Diplomatic conventions have purpose and meaning. The protocol persists because it is an integral part of the diplomatic encounter. Practices and ceremonies that have their origins in the European court have retained their relevance, and have been transformed to serve the modern international society.[2]

Diplomats are social agents who conduct their business according to a distinctive code of behavior and accepted rules of the game.[3] There is no clear boundary between form and substance; the formal and the informal interact with each other, as the ceremonial and the substantial are bounded together. The formality and the ritualistic style of diplomacy are there to fulfil an intended purpose, namely, to facilitate dialogue and to serve mutual interests. Thus, conventions have been incorporated into the foundational propositions about diplomatic norms of behavior that constitute the diplomatic culture.

— •◦• —

Diplomats have duties that they perform formally. This is possible only by the most firmly established diplomatic convention—the continued

23

observance of the inviolability of the diplomatic envoy. Both Rosier and Grotius asserted that the diplomat's safety serves the public good. The immunity granted to envoys created metaphorical islands of ambassadorial security amid international anarchy. Diplomatic activity must be protected and not be subject to constraint. Immunity from the civil and criminal jurisdiction of the receiving state should be granted, and security has to be provided to diplomatic envoys, as well as to the premises and property of embassies.[4]

Although abused from time to time, immunity is a necessity rather than a privilege. The guarantee of freedom of movement, and safety from all forms of interference, became the custom in the late middle ages, enshrined in the civil and canon law. In 1414, Henry V of England declared the violation of safe conduct an act of high treason against the crown.[5] And from the seventeenth century on, juristic safeguards began to replace religious taboos and voluntary reciprocity.

Grotius's revolutionary assertion that the law of nations would remain valid even if God did not exist attests to the fact that international law progressed by the measure of its distance from religious sanctity. Civil and judicial principles advanced by philosophers and theologians like Grotius replaced Christian canon. Thus, the law of nations took roots along the law of nature, though international law became universal only in the last century.

Reciprocity, convention, and international law were not always enough to protect diplomats. Until the Middle Ages and the early modern period, the exchange of hostages to guarantee the safety of the diplomat was a frequent occurrence.[6] The immunity of diplomats had ultimately survived the challenge of revolutionary regimes, beginning with the French Revolution. The Enlightenment and the rise of Liberalism did not shield diplomats from attacks on their privileges on both sides of the Atlantic. Indeed, the immunity of diplomats has been abused in modern time more than in any period in history.[7]

In the nineteenth century, the triumph of functionalism, which restricted immunities and privileges to what ambassadors needed in order to accomplish their tasks, was, on the whole, beneficial to diplomatic reputation. The restrictive approach to diplomatic privileges was augmented by the Vienna Convention of 1961. The convention reserved intact what is essential for free and proper diplomatic activity—the exemption from both the civil and criminal jurisdiction of the receiving country. In addition, it has a duty to protect the mission and its premises, and to guarantee the freedom of both movement and communication. But, it is the duty of all persons enjoying these privileges to respect the laws and the regulations of the receiving state.[8] Such immunities, of course, did not reduce the temptation to violate them, particularly by authoritarian regimes.

——— •◆• ———

The standard tasks of a permanent mission have an enduring existence, since the interpretation and meaning of the diplomatic practice do not change much. Diplomats represent their country symbolically and substantially, gather information, convey messages, and conduct negotiations.[9] Though there is not much debate as to the diplomat's main duties, traditionalists are under the pressure of the challenges of a fragmented world with a plurality of authorities and an expanding international agenda. Diplomatic envoys are called on to respond more vigorously to the voluntary activity of nongovernmental organizations and private citizens, as well as to invest more efforts in public diplomacy and commercial affairs.[10] Diplomats maintain a skeptical view of such an inclusive perspective of diplomacy, as it is difficult to assess the value of private activity and what is gained exactly from unofficial contacts.

The diplomat is far from being a civil servant in chains and has wider scope to maneuver than is usually portrayed. The chief function of ambassadors is to secure good relations toward their countries, and to promote their political, economic, and cultural interests. They take it upon themselves to interpret for their governments the views of the country to which they are posted, enabling it to make a reasonable judgment of the situation and to act accordingly. Ambassadors are generally empowered to sign international agreements and to deal with all issues that may arise between two states. Evidently, only a resident diplomat can accomplish the tasks of representing, negotiating, and reporting.[11]

Diplomats are often portrayed as practitioners who have been robbed of their prime expertise, namely, negotiation. There is, in fact, no appropriate substitute for the skilled diplomat. If, to follow the advice given by Guicciardini, Richelieu, and Callières, he is able to wait for the ripe moment, change course according to circumstances, and make suitable concessions.[12] This is especially the case in our era, which is rife with presumptions about new and unconventional forms of diplomacy. Negotiations are integral to the essence of diplomacy, and are best conducted by its chief practitioner.

Diplomats are at present haunted by the new demands of the telecommunication revolution with its varied and ever accumulating devices, and the potentiality of reducing human encounter to a fax, an electronic text, or even only a tweet. But, from the bewilderment of Palmerston at the introduction of the telegraph, to the recent miracles of communication that have changed the spatial and temporal dimensions of humanity, the doomsday of diplomacy is yet to arrive.

Communication by telephone and telegraph impelled Satow to comment that swiftness in deliberation carries the risk of obstructing reflection and consultation, while vital matters are left to hasty decisions and irreversible mistakes.[13] The impact of the media on diplomacy has yet to be carefully analyzed. Undoubtedly, the vast amount of information has made international reality less comprehensible, presenting a challenge to human cognitive capabilities, but it is doubtful whether beyond location, logistics, and form, it has changed the substance and essence of diplomacy. The diplomat's desk has been changed, new skills have to be acquired, and methods adjusted. There is, perhaps, also a mounting "digital divide," not only between nations, but also between old and young diplomats. All these can still be coordinated, and technologically "supported."

The availability of information via the Internet raises serious questions as to relevance and reliability. Communicating by e-mails, or conferring by cellular phones and video-conferences, is accompanied by a loss of discretion and reduced possibility of fully preserving diplomatic records or reconstructing them in the future. The computerization of diplomatic procedures does not endear them to practitioners, and will certainly not be viewed favorably by historians in the future.[14]

The media are now integrated into foreign affairs, and displayed before the general public. This puts demands on the professional diplomats to be performers, to make the case for their countries openly, reaching a wide audience. These rituals of necessity affect values and influence policies to a limited extent. Public opinion, however important, cannot replace either reality or historical patterns. The impact of public opinion, particularly on negotiation, is ambivalent at best. Abba Eban observed that "public opinion often inhibits the slow ripening of wisdom."[15] Excessive preoccupation with the media and public diplomacy could only be a distraction, and leads to hollow rhetoric and unnecessary competition with nonstate actors. Multiple audiences with different values and interests are usually the gateway to unintended consequences.[16]

As for the relations between the diplomat and the correspondent, tradition is changing by small paces. The courtship of journalists carries risks to the reputation of the diplomat. And it is hard to conceal the fact that they have competing roles—disclosure, but not necessarily for the same purpose.[17] Gathering information and reporting remain essential and enduring tasks of the diplomat. Being only one among other agents in this mission has proved to be purely beneficial. The professional diplomat may not always be viewed as honorable, but is no longer considered a spy. Callières and Hedley Bull made the same observation about the importance of diplomats in this regard. Diplomats are skilled in gathering the specific information that is essential to the conduct of international politics. A mere account of facts does not amount to much. Diplomats must conceal nothing in their reports, and be exact and faithful.[18]

— ••• —

Diplomatic ceremonies are portrayed as petty rituals that take a heavy toll on diplomats' time, confining them in grotesque bonds. A frustrated King Charles II referred to Hyde's guide to etiquette as a book of "inscriptions, subscriptions and superscriptions." President Truman complained that "protocol and striped pants give me a pain in the neck."[19] Indeed, the republican claim that diplomatic ceremonies are archaic and devoid of reason gained substantial ground. But diplomatic ceremonies survived the onslaught of Bolshevik dogmatism, abuse by totalitarian regimes on the radical right, criticism from strategic pundits during the Cold War era and the pretentious rhetoric of liberals.

Rituals and ceremonies are of importance, if not of necessity. Callières, always prudent in his approach to diplomacy, paid attention to such matters, and Jules Cambon was right to observe that "all is not devoid of sense in these solemn frivolities."[20] First, the rules of diplomacy that are followed ceremonially facilitate diplomatic exchange, establish order, and clarify ambiguities. They also make it possible to present messages with dignity and in a commonly accepted manner.[21]

Diplomatic rituals of the past involved certain privileges, both desired and resented, although royal indulgence has since been abandoned and replaced by functional ones. Diplomatic ceremonial of the past served an important purpose—it was an explicit demonstration of the power, international rank, and influence of the state. The kings of France were the envy of European courts, as the splendor of the prince was the greatness of his state.

Court ceremonies were designed to impress foreign envoys—and in the case of the Chinese and Ottoman Empires to demonstrate their subjugation and inferiority. This was the case with Roman triumphal processions and Byzantine intricacies, which set the example for the court society of Europe. The Byzantines, being masters of rituals, displayed images of real or presumed wealth and splendor to impress envoys of the imperial power, and to popularize the emperor's image as a holy and universal prince. Ambassadors had to succumb to a "posture of awe, humility, and submission." They were hurried through the labyrinths of palaces to the roar of mechanical gilded lions, and the song of golden birds. The sublime and the luxurious were deployed as a diplomatic trap.[22]

The city-states of Italy followed the oriental and Byzantine traditions, adding splendor and color to the entry of envoys, transforming the ambassadorial procession into an entertainment and a public banquet. In China and the Ottoman Empires, court ceremonies were rituals of humiliation and intimidation. The foreign ambassador was forced to kneel and kiss the sultan's robe, and to declaim his address before a motionless and abusing sultan. The Chinese practice was no less humiliating. After being escorted by the imperial cortege, ambassadors had to follow the ritual of the kowtow—to kneel three times, knocking their head on the ground.[23]

The most significant change in the structure and aim of diplomatic ceremonies was their transformation from rituals of domination to those of convenience and formal state equality. No longer is diplomatic ceremony part of the configuration of power and the struggle between monarchs. Instead it serves two important social functions—a purposeful delay of proceedings, and the structuring of distance, an element essential to the diplomatic encounter.

———— .•. ————

Georg Simmel was the first to define distance as a principle of social interaction, claiming that human beings begin to be "social" when there is a distance between them.[24] In his monumental writings on European civilization and court society, Norbert Elias empirically perfected the notion of social distance.[25] Manners were always integral to any civilizing process, constructing forms of conduct and habits of self-control. Ceremonies and etiquette became essential instruments of the distribution of power, and the fierce competition for status and prestige in the European courts. Every individual had to take part in a "ghostly *perpetuum mobile*," if one wanted to preserve his standing in court, being constantly attentive to every nuance and detail. Etiquette served as a mechanism of distancing oneself from others in order to acquire greater esteem and power; ceremony established the hierarchy of power.

The diplomatic ceremony inherited from the European court replaced the distance between classes with a different one—the configured distance between diplomats. The diplomatic ceremonial is a purposeful delay, and serves as a preliminary act of mutual observation. In the past, monarchs and their functionaries needed time in order to inquire about the credentials of incoming envoys, and to estimate the extent of their powers. Prudence called for an exact judgment before surrendering anything in the ensuing proceedings. On the other hand, incoming diplomats had the chance of being acquainted with their interlocutors in order to delineate their first steps in the encounter. Furthermore, ceremonies build a detachment that distinguishes diplomatic encounters from mere intimate human gatherings.

It took quite a long time until court rituals had been transformed into frameworks of convenience, and aristocratic manners were perfected as conventions. Protocol, ceremony and ritual are terms that are used interchangeably. There are differences between them, but all three serve one ultimate purpose—facilitating diplomatic communication. The protocol is more than etiquette. It is an accepted code of conduct that imposes reciprocal respect, mediates hostility, and regulates encounters in a civilized way. The diplomatic protocol solved the problem of precedence, allotting "to each his proper place in the political and administrative structure."[26] It became a mixture of good manners and common sense that provides balance to the diplomatic platform. As a universal code, the protocol assists in isolating cultural differences to a certain degree.

The diplomatic protocol orients diplomats from the moment they reach their posts and present their credentials until their departure. These "stage directions," which refer to ceremonial dress, titles and receptions, table plans and conference seatings, still retain their functions. The protocol has established a diplomatic tradition, any deviation from which may signify an intentional insult.[27] The diplomatic code achieves another purpose that often escapes notice. It serves as a public commitment to the norms of international society, maintaining the equality of states as far as immediate diplomatic procedures are concerned. The protocol puts negotiators on equal terms, and respects their national dignity.

For all the fetishism of etiquette and ceremony, they still preserve their connection with the primary functions of diplomacy. Rationality of procedures and the "disenchantment" of the world that modernity has brought, have modified the rituals of honor, but have not eliminated them. At Westphalia, the first six months of negotiations were wasted deciding how parties would be seated and in what order they would enter. Three centuries later, at the Potsdam Conference, Churchill, Stalin, and Truman were still unable to agree on who should enter the conference room first.[28] Harold Nicolson detested "dressing up for official ceremonies in full uniform and gold lace, little sword getting between his legs." Callières advised diplomats instead, to attempt to speak to the prince without ceremony.[29]

Some ceremonies tend to be ritualistic. Rituals are repetitive, symbolic, and retain sacrosanct elements. The purification of heralds was prevalent in ancient times. The conclusion of treaties in the diplomacy of the Ancient Near East involved making sacrifices to the gods and swearing oaths, symbolizing the divine commitment undertaken, and the punishment attached to a breach of the treaty. In Rome, diplomatic rituals were performed by the college *fetials*. Papal *legates* wore red robes to set them apart from other envoys.[30] Diplomatic ceremonies as rituals of repetition appeal to the senses, not only to the intellect. They carry the logic of a self-fulfilling prophecy—the hope for desired conclusions.

4

—— ·◆· ——

The Diplomatic Forum

THE DIPLOMATIC FORUM is the "place" where diplomats act as representatives of their states. It is a public sphere, demarcated and ordained
as such. The diplomatic forum has some of the properties of the traditional battlefield, at least until the twentieth century. The battlefield
always possessed the dual faces of Janus—enshrined and glorified, but
also surrounded by doom, defeat, and death. Both diplomatic forum
and battlefield are the court of fateful decisions, places of both rewards
and punishments.

The diplomatic forum has a prescribed structure and rules that
transform a gathering from a mere aggregate of persons into being a
purposeful social interaction. As a diplomatic marketplace it occurs in
varied settings and locations: palaces, dining halls, conference rooms,
hotel lobbies, and even cemeteries. In the past, diplomats conducted
their encounters in temples, bridges, and spas.[1] Receptions and official
meals in the royal palaces of the Ancient Near East were places in which
the quality of the relations between kingdoms was revealed, as notables
and envoys dined together, exchanged gifts, and carefully observed each
other. Olympia and Delphi were designated by the Greeks as forums of
Hellenic festivity, and as places to sanctify important treaties.[2]

The hostility between the kings of France and England in the fifteenth century forced them to carefully choose the places of their diplomatic exchanges. In 1475 they agreed to meet at the heads of their
forces in full battle array, while envoys passed from one to the other until
an arrangement was reached. Commynes provides a detailed description of the way Picquigny was chosen for the meeting between Louis XI
and Edward IV, king of England, at that time. The crafty French built a

bridge over the river Somme with a wooden lattice in the middle, and bars running across both sides of the bridge to hinder any person from crossing it to either side.[3]

Diplomacy flourished in the seventeenth century, inflaming the struggle over precedence, and heightening the ambivalence toward the resident embassies. The negotiations of the Peace of Westphalia were conducted at two sites, Münster and Osnabruck, to avoid disputes over precedence. And in European royal palaces, distinction was made between reception rooms—one quarter for relatively intimate social intercourse, and another ceremonial section to serve for official visits.[4]

It was a continental habit of the nineteenth century to meet in spas, the best known among them being Baden-Baden, Carlsbad, and Marienbad. The spa was a crowded place, where diplomats and politicians had their meetings under the public eyes, yet availing themselves excellent amenities. In these unofficial settings Bismarck held two important meetings with Napoleon III at Biarritz, and Cavour conspired with Napoleon against Austria at Plombières in July 1858.[5]

With the expansion of conference diplomacy, meeting places became a matter of prestige and expediency. The Hague in the Netherlands and Geneva in Switzerland became prime meeting places for international conferences. Hegemonial powers usually established their prerogatives in such decisions, as was the case with the United States after the Second World War.

——— •◆• ———

Forums are invented for the conduct of diplomatic encounters, providing a setting of both distance and intimacy. Distance is a necessity when the intimacy of the diplomatic gathering contradicts the definition of the social situation, namely, a dialogue conducted between enemies, rivals, or at least in a state of disagreement. To some extent ceremonies and rituals bridge the gap between the intimacy of the encounter and its confrontational nature. Diplomatic ceremonial instills a chilly decorum between the parties. This is, perhaps, the only way citizens are capable emotionally of bestowing legitimacy on their representatives in dealing with the enemy.[6] Apparently, an element of estrangement is conducive to the diplomatic dialogue. It advances mutual coordination and limits the scope for misunderstanding.[7]

The number of participants in any diplomatic encounter influences its structure, the rules that apply and its ultimate results. A dyad usually ties each of its participants to a common fate. The secession of one destroys the whole. The dyad, as a rule, abolishes rank and hierarchy, and—at least from a social point of view—places the individuals concerned on equal terms. The dyad is intimate, confidential, and risky. It also arouses jealousy among those who are not taking part in it. The dyad provides maximal room for individuality, and thus it is especially suitable for diplomats who desire to be recognized for their talents.[8] A dyad can result in personal commitments that may not be supported either by governments or even by senior diplomats. A case in point is the Treaty of Björko, an alliance between Russia and Germany signed by Wilhelm II and Czar Nikolai II in July 1905. It was a futile exercise in personal diplomacy that was rejected by both Russian and German diplomats and disappeared into oblivion.[9]

A summit meeting between heads of state, a dyad in principle, is the most resented forum, unanimously criticized by professional diplomats. Commynes spoke for many when he asserted that ". . . great princes, who are desirous to preserve a more than ordinary friendship, ought never see each other." They should better employ wise emissaries. Harold Nicolson, who was witness to the negotiations at Versailles, commented that the habit of personal contact between statesmen is one of the worst diplomatic inventions; there was nothing more damaging to precision and good diplomacy than summitries that ended in "the horrors of vagueness."[10]

Summitry as a tête-à-tête meeting is viewed as an "uncontrolled" encounter that circumvents diplomatic procedure. The difficulty of reconstructing summit deliberations is an additional failing. Pavel Palazchenko, translator for Gorbachev and Shevardnadze, admits that interpretations are never complete, and their exactitude is a matter of loyalty—either to the truth, the language, or the leader involved.[11]

Summits create great expectations, amplify small faults, and expose the limitations of leaders. The dependence on personal rapport and domestic considerations only adds to the confusion. Being the court of last resort, diplomacy at the highest level makes compromise difficult and results irreversible. The decline of the ambassadorial role distances the opportunity for the meticulous preparation that could have saved many summits from failure.[12]

One of the most notorious summit meetings was held in Vienna in June 1961, between President Kennedy and Nikita Khrushchev. The President consulted the best experts on Russia—Averell Harriman, Charles Bohlen, George Kennan, and the ambassador to Moscow, Llewellyn Thompson. He also sought the counsel of De Gaulle, who told him "don't get into a fight. Rise above it. Have some fun." Kennedy was confident that the meeting would reduce the tension between the two superpowers, and that the two leaders would be able to confer on issues of importance. In the two encounters, held respectively in the

American and the Russian Embassies, the combative general secretary utterly ignored Kennedy's efforts to establish greater rapport, and the exchange between the two leaders ended in heated argument and antagonism. Rather than a discussion of matters of substance, it was a planned assault on the president.

Kennedy left the summit meeting frustrated, complaining that Khrushchev had treated him like a little boy. He admitted that it was the "roughest thing in my life." Shaken by his experience at the summit meeting, and troubled by his own performance, he was now resolved not to be bullied into any concessions. Bohlen concluded that the talks "conditioned" the president for the crises on Berlin and Cuba.[13] In retrospect, it seems that what Khrushchev gained in Vienna was lost in October 1962.

Politicians and heads of state are no substitute for the accumulated experience of professional diplomats. Agreements concluded by statesmen must be maintained, nurtured, and subjected to periodic assessment. Prolonged negotiations and meticulous preparations usually precede the conclusion of an agreement's final details. Summit meetings, however, are suitable and necessary in times of crisis, though they cannot serve as a permanent substitute for continuous diplomatic activity. The great complexity of international affairs suggests caution about the prospects for a solution through meetings between heads of state. No doubt, professional diplomats prefer the calculated routine of diplomatic procedures.

The advance of multilateralism has found its prime venue in conferences and permanent international organizations. The conference is the most regulated diplomatic forum, a sphere managed by exact rules of procedure. It is a structured encounter, with its own logistics, tactics, and objectives. Detailed preparations regulate the date and place of the conference, its agenda, the composition of delegations, and their credentials. Informal explorations lead to formal procedures—the appointment of a secretariat, the debates in plenary sessions where diplomats perform publicly, and the work in closed committees, until delegates compose a draft and agree on a final resolution.[14]

Apparently, the larger the group, the less intimate it becomes, a situation that either strengthens or disturbs the encounter. In a conference, as in all multilateral meetings, responsibility is dispersed, and tactics are less detectable. And the effort to bind different issues together may result in ambiguity and delays.

The significance and meaning of a diplomatic encounter depends on its properties, in particular whether it is occasional or preplanned.[15] An encounter of this kind is rarely a spontaneous gathering. It is designed to achieve a well-defined purpose, though this is not always the case. The reputable writers on diplomacy have furnished the professional diplomat with elaborate counsels in this regard. Francis Bacon emphasized first impressions: "the start or first performance is all." Callières instructed the diplomat to be in full command of himself, control his passions, and carefully study the situation. Satow stressed empathy, and the ability of the diplomat to put himself in the position of the person with whom he was negotiating. While for Nicolson precision, both moral and intellectual, was essential, other commentators related to the importance of patience and perseverance, good temper, and honesty.[16] Threats, inducements, and deceptions are criticized, or ignored altogether.

The necessity of diplomats to present prescribed positions naturally displays the metaphor of the diplomat as actor. Callières and Wicquefort followed, in this regard, their predecessors in the Renaissance. As a matter of fact, Bertolt Brecht's conception of alienation provides the most exact meaning of the diplomat's performance. The actor, according to Brecht, should not fully identify with the character he is playing. On the contrary, he must remain calculated and detached even when he is playing passionate parts.[17] In the same way, the diplomat has to be aware of his dual role—as representative, and as an individual.

The notion of the diplomat as actor leads directly to the investigation of the role of gestures and emotions in the diplomatic dialogue. Diplomats have rich nonverbal repertoires for expressing approval, anger, or nonacceptance, in order to indicate their positions on a given issue. Despite the fact that they have defined terms of reference, their room for maneuvering is greater than expected. Diplomats, however, must see to it that the words and impressions they convey are compatible and consistent with their governments' intentions.[18]

Talleyrand is frequently quoted as saying that "Above all, avoid an excess of enthusiasm." Callières complements this view, stressing that the display of emotions is an impediment to negotiations. But Bismarck used his calculated rage and "decided impatience" to a great effect. Contemporary literature on diplomacy is beginning to consider emotions as another tool in the diplomatic repertoire.[19]

—— ••• ——

Diplomatic encounters are either carefully planned, or occasional. The latter are generally not properly arranged, are of short duration and hardly constructive. This is the case with most state visits, summits, coronations, and funerals. These are mainly forums of symbolic gestures, although they are sometimes considered to be confidence-building or the beginning of reconciliation.[20]

Occasional encounters may prove to be grotesque or even bordering on the absurd. Douglas Busk recalls that as a young diplomatist in the British embassy in Tokyo in 1941, he had to face a Japanese messenger hurriedly proclaiming that he had come to declare a state of war between Japan and Britain. Abba Eban described the presentation of his credentials as ambassador of Israel to the United States in the following way: "the President [Truman] feared I might follow tradition and actually declaim the text . . . he snatched the document from my hands and said, 'let's cut out this crap and have a real talk.'" Not that meetings in other parts of the world provided a more suitable ambiance. We find the following entry in Piers Dixon's diary on his meeting with Ibn-Saud, King of Saudi-Arabia, in February 1945: "behind his chair stood an interpreter, the astrologer, two food-testers and two guards armed with daggers and revolvers."[21] Other encounters may be intentional in purpose, but counterproductive. At a meeting held in January 2010 between Israel's deputy foreign minister, Danny Ayalon, and the ambassador of Turkey, Israeli officials sat the latter on a lower sofa and invited camerapeople to capture his supposed public humiliation. The Turks asked for an apology, and the deputy minister acquiesced without delay.[22]

— .◆. —

Wicqueford commented that "there is no rule to be given for the manner of negotiation." The literature, though, on its conduct and methods abound, as negotiations are the most continuous and reciprocal diplomatic encounter.[23] They provide a moment of truth, and are, perhaps, the most creative diplomatic activity, if successful. The merits of secrecy, the ripeness of the situations, and the clash of cultures involved, are recurrent themes in the literature on negotiation. Bacon and Callières praised the advantages of the person-to-person encounter. Thus, skillful diplomats have the opportunity to observe accurately those with whom they treat, and adapt themselves to changing circumstances. Nicolson, on the other hand, trusted written exchanges that ensure lucidity and precision.[24]

Negotiations are often conducted between parties with no shared values or worldviews. The attempt to preserve clarity and shared meanings is a task not easily achieved. Problems of interpretation and semantic confusion are recurrent. The universality of diplomatic conventions is of merit, but does not constitute an ultimate remedy for the clash of cultures.[25] The secrecy of negotiation became a matter of contention only with the introduction of the idea of open diplomacy during the First World War. Diplomats are fascinated by secrecy, and are united in regarding it as being of the utmost importance. De Vera, Callièrs, and

Pecquet apotheosized secrecy as the "life" of negotiations. Abba Eban remarked, in a rather understated note, that it is reasonable to regret the eclipse of secrecy.[26]

An obsession with secretiveness was prevalent in the Middle Ages and the Renaissance. And Nevile Henderson, who served in the British Embassy in St. Petersburg at the beginning of the twentieth century, recalled that it took nine keys to get from the embassy's front door to the last drawer of the safe in the chancery. A diametrically different and rare example is that of Edward Grey and Paul Cambon, the French ambassador to London, who showed each other their record of a conversation between them before reporting to their respective governments.[27]

The essence of the matter is whether publicity may hamper diplomatic efforts to reach agreements on essential international issues. An appropriate measure of secrecy, particularly during negotiations, is essential. This is a proposition argued not on moral grounds, but on the basis of expediency and common sense. Anthony Eden mused to President Roosevelt in 1942, that the best way is "to reach open covenants secretly arrived at," to which the president cheerfully agreed.[28]

5

—— •>• ——

Credentials of Words

THE DIPLOMATIC DIALOGUE is based on the familiar and shared termi-
nology of diplomatic representatives. Written instructions to ambassadors appeared quite early in the history of diplomacy. Hedley Bull
complimented diplomats for being experts in precise and accurate communication, detecting and conveying the nuances of the international
dialogue. Machiavelli always attended to the expedient, warned envoys
that they would be judged, above all, by their dispatches, one among
their arsenal of survival.[1]

The art of presentation was always central in the diplomatic mission, constituting a prelude to a successful dialogue and mutual understanding. In ancient time, the Renaissance and early modern history,
oratorical talents were considered essential requirement of the diplomat. Harold Nicolson, though, insisted in all his diplomatic writings that
diplomacy was a written craft, not the art of conversation, highlighting
Bacon's dictum that writing makes "an exact man."[2]

The symbiosis between art, literature in particular, and diplomacy is
a notable phenomenon. Accomplished poets, artists, and philosophers
have served as professional diplomats. The summit of this achievement
is reserved, perhaps, for French and Latin diplomats.[3] Dante, Petrarch,
and Boccaccio in Italy, Chaucer, Marlowe, and Chesterfield in England,
were courtiers and diplomats, like many other humanists. Rubens, the
famous painter, played a major role in Anglo-Spanish relations. Machiavelli and Grotius are notable among philosophers. By 1712, Leibniz was
in the pay of five different courts. Rousseau, Hume, and Locke served
minor diplomatic missions.[4]

Literary achievement was dear to many diplomatists. The British diplomat Piers Dixon wrote in his diary: "Literature and creation are all that life is worth living for." Robert Vansittart's inspiration included playwriting and poetry. In his obituary to George Kennan, the historian John Gaddis commented that Kennan saw himself as a literary figure: "he would have loved to have been a poet, a novelist."[5]

Literature and diplomacy were inseparable in the lives of Callières and Nicolson. Bismarck is generally complimented for his literary style. In the case of Nicolson, the combination of literary work and diplomacy led to a serious crisis of identity. Feeling bored with the foreign office, he was aware that he could not do much better at literature. His shortcomings as a writer, enumerated in Edmund Wilson's review of his literary work, greatly troubled him.[6]

Combining literature and diplomacy, French and Latin diplomats brought both to the highest level. Paul Claudel served as his country's ambassador to Japan, Belgium, and the United States between the world wars. He claimed a complete separation between his poetry and his ambassadorial mission. For Pablo Neruda, diplomacy appears to have served as a cover for political activity, and as a distraction from poetry. Neruda gained entry to the Chilean foreign ministry due to patronage, as was the case for many other artists, when a friend introduced him to Chile's foreign minister. When asked: "where do you want to go, Pablo?" his answer was Rangoon. It was the only name he remembered when vacancies were enumerated.[7]

A notable case of a both poet and a diplomat was that of Alexis Saint-Léger.[8] A poet of repute, under the nom de plume Saint-John Perse, he was appointed General Secretary of the French Foreign Office with the rank of Ambassador in 1933. In the case of Léger, literature and diplomacy were quite separated, though the subtleties of his language and his aloofness created some detachment from others. He published no verse between 1924 and his exile from France in the early 1940s.

— .•. —

Diplomatic correspondence obeys strict conventions, and its style is traditionally "stiff, cold, formal, and dignified." Language, of course, determines meaning and tone, *Stylus virum arguit* (Our style betrays us). Salvador de Madariaga claimed that language was an expression of national character.[9] The traditional forms of correspondence—the *note verbale* and the memorandum are subject to agreed rules of presentation. They are all on the record, and even the *note-verbale* is a written document.[10]

Diplomatic correspondence tends to be ritualistic, using phrases that repeat themselves. Each document is a device for a calculated purpose. The carefully chosen words serve "the unspoken assumption," that they indicate the degree of commitment of all parties. In accordance with "gentlemen's" courtesy in the past, the language of diplomatic correspondence was high-sounding and laudatory. Today it has been replaced by a simpler, more functional style, though it is still distant from the current decline of linguistic discipline.[11] The reserved tone, the guarded understatements, and the precise code of the diplomatic language are useful, if not necessary, particularly in negotiations. Yet, to a certain extent, speaking thus is like "wearing a disguise." Diplomats are exceptional, in this regard, as part of their task is to be constantly vigilant regarding the clarity of their intentions.

Words carry significance, and diplomats must weigh them with great precision, as "they are part of the substance, not the form, of the diplomatic enterprise."[12] As much as diplomatic texts are unattractive, the traditional forms of correspondence are necessary for establishing a linguistic common ground. The world of mass communications, popular demagoguery and absolutist phraseology is the furthest from the understatements and nuances of diplomatic language. There is no coherent and reasonable alternative to such ritualistic elegance, particularly in the absence of a diplomatic lingua franca, and the semantic confusion that prevails.[13]

In a world of linguistic diversity, any assumption of universality is highly questionable. Languages, as an integral part of culture, attest to different ontologies, and have a variety of meanings of legal terms, ethics, and political concepts. Indeed, the principal terms of the diplomatic dialogue—compromise, concession, peace, and alliance—are comprehended and interpreted differently. Constructive ambiguity, dear to the drafters of treaties, is no substitute for the gaps in the construction of different diplomatic realities.[14]

A shared lingua franca, with its nuances and connotations, was no guarantee of consent, even within the *res publica christiana*. The diplomatic language during the Middle Ages and the Renaissance was Latin, but it was declining in the seventeenth century. The treaties of Westphalia were conducted in Latin, though French was already gaining dominance. French was employed throughout the Congress of Vienna in 1815. On the aftermath of the First World War, English was accepted as having equal standing with French. The League of Nations adopted either French or English in its discussions, with a consecutive translation of each speech into the other language. Apparently, political hegemony affects the choice of diplomatic languages. English has emerged in the last century as a global lingua franca, in what seems to be a civilizational cycle.[15]

As it is but illusive to expect universal agreement on shared meanings and values, the semantic domain of diplomatic conventions remains the preferred platform of international dialogue. Using such phrases as, one "cannot remain indifferent to," or "view in concern," limits the scope of misunderstanding, providing room for maneuver before approaching the last resort of force.[16] A knowledge of foreign languages, which was common among diplomats of previous generations, is still of importance. A notable case was that of Ernest Satow, who represented England in China and Japan, and spoke the languages of both.[17] Insistence on "clarity and economy of expression" is imperative for sound diplomatic practice. Words that are precise, purposive, and civilized are preferable to metaphors and elliptical phrasing. The enduring truth is that the diplomat must be a person of words.[18]

—— •·• ——

Representation and presentation, two of the prime functions of the diplomat, are interconnected. The symbolic and formal aspects of representation establish international legitimacy and are the legal source of relations between states. The ambassador of the past represented his sovereign, and was thus obliged, first and foremost, to protect the dignity and interests of his master.[19] The direct consequence of this was the fierce struggle over precedence that continued well into the late eighteenth century. Another bone of contention was the order of signature on the conclusion of international treaties. Precedence became an acute problem in the seventeenth and eighteenth centuries, with the establishment of the diplomatic residence, and the shifts in the European balance of power.

The fiercest struggles over precedence took place during the rise of France to preeminence, and the simultaneous decline of Spain as a great power. There was a notorious clash in London in September 1661, between the French and Spanish entourages, in contest of the order of entry into the King's meeting chambers. After a street battle with drawn swords, the Spaniards won a short-lived precedence. The incident led to a rupture in the relations between France and Spain. Louis XIV, threatening war, forced Spain to apologize and accord precedence to the French ambassador at the Bourbon Courts, while in other kingdoms precedence would be decided by the date of arrival.[20]

Setting the *problematique* of precedence was one of the achievements of the Congress of Vienna. The Congress set one standard for diplomatic ranks, and established precedence according to the date of ambassadors' arrival at the seat of their mission.[21] Diplomatic precedence was no longer a matter for formal dispute. Precedence could now be gained and lost in the marketplace of international politics. Envoys, who are vested with the authority to speak for their country, are judged according to their professional performance, not by the prestige of their sovereign.[22]

Representation at contemporary international affairs is complex, as many societies are ethnically and politically divided, and national identities fragmented. Diplomats have to cope with the widening gap between formal representation and the fractured entity they are representing. What are the dividing lines between the state, civil society, and other advocacy groups who compete for different policy goals? While diplomats have lost their exclusive role as representatives, they are still honored or attacked on the basis of an all-encompassing definition of their prerogatives. Discrepancies of this kind, particularly taking into consideration the limited mandate given to diplomats, are obviously punishable. It is the closing of a full circle that goes back to historical periods when diplomatic envoys were vulnerable, simply because they fulfilled their duty as representatives of their country.[23]

Presentation, on the other hand, depends on the skill and appearance of the diplomat. Callières was of the opinion that a man of letters would make a better ambassador. Eloquence is necessary, but not sufficient. The act of presentation is framed by a duality. As representatives, diplomats stand outside themselves, but at the same time they must maintain their individuality. It is a movement "from exclusive focus on the actor to a view which brings the stage into the forefront of the picture."[24] There is a tension between the ambassadorial duty to carry out the instructions given to them, and the extent to which they are allowed to convey meanings beyond the written word but according to circumstances. It is a constant interplay between the objective and the subjective, "to make present the unrepresentable and to 'see' what cannot be seen."[25]

6

——— ·•· ———

Diplomats and Their Milieu

DIPLOMACY IS A way of life, from apprenticeship to retirement. Throughout, the diplomat dwells in a milieu which is socially artificial, but very real in its demands. As aristocratic privileges have been lost, diplomats now face a domineering bureaucracy, while struggling to reconcile their various roles, abroad and at home.

The aristocracy dominated the diplomatic apparatus well into the twentieth century. Members of the upper classes were bound for diplomacy as a matter of social standing, wealth, and their contractual relation with sovereigns. It was a setting of convenience and mutual dependency that was exploited by both sides. The alliance between the monarchy and the nobility established the tradition of privileges and courtly manners as the foundation of diplomatic practice. The hostility to the exclusive milieu of diplomacy went hand in hand with the progressive decline of the aristocracy, and the separation from social class allowed merit to be the primary criterion in the choice of envoys.[1]

Until the state took responsibility for expenses, wealth was a necessary requirement for sustaining ambassadorial hospitality, and payment for junior staff. Gifts furnished by sovereigns were not enough as compensation. The rising cost of embassies induced monarchs to sell titles in order to raise money to finance important posts. Lawrence Stone provides the following description of the needs of an English nobleman aspiring to fulfil his diplomatic obligations: "to equip himself for the post he had to have horses, coaches, sumptuous clothes for himself, and rich liveries for his attendants. Once abroad, he had to maintain his horde of servants and attendants, to entertain lavishly. For these enormous costs the English crown made only a grudging contribution."[2]

The memoirs of British diplomats of the last century make it clear that a privileged family was a primary requisite for a diplomatic career. The pattern of being educated in a public school, and then Oxford or Cambridge, is recurrent in the records of the Foreign Office. Diplomats were considered to embody the ideals of a gentleman—in manners, loyalty to king and country, and in the pursuit of gentlemanly excellence, particularly as sportsmen.[3] David Kelley complained in his memoirs of his alienation in the Foreign Office, due to not having been educated in a public school, but rather in a London day-school. It was Herbert Warren, the President of Magdalen College, who secured his nomination to the foreign service.[4] Already Wicquefort and Callières were of the opinion that the nobility does not, necessarily, make for good diplomats. And Nicolson pointed out that some of the earliest and most able English diplomats had come from humble origins, and that sound diplomacy was the invention of the middle class.[5]

With the rise of foreign ministries, bureaucracies replaced social class as the regulators of diplomatic life. In addition to the routine complaint about excessive privileges, criticism of diplomats now focused on the dysfunctions of the diplomatic service. Richelieu's decree of 1626 demanding that external affairs be concentrated within one ministry founded a pattern that lasted well into the twentieth century. The new bureaucracies of the eighteenth century devised the standards for the operating procedures of the foreign service, though patronage lasted until the twentieth century.[6]

Every foreign service operates as a divided bureaucracy, separating the home ministry from the staffs in scattered embassies. The expansion of foreign ministries in the last century made them the target of a populist resentment and political skepticism. Bureaucratic routine became the symbol for lack of foresight, paucity of originality, and absence of inventiveness.[7]

Routine, as much as it is nonheroic, enhances both structural and political stability. The foreign services of Europe and North America managed to reform and even revolutionize their bureaucratic operating standards. The United States, after operating for a long time with a completely neglected foreign service, employed in 2010 a staff of 30,260, among them more than 12,000 professional officers representing it in 260 missions.[8] However, reforms were introduced with neither real constituency, nor with public interest in diplomacy or diplomats.

— •◦• —

The training of diplomats, it seems, will never be satisfactory. The study of certain skills cannot replace the slow adaptation to the diplomatic role, both social and professional. But, what makes a good diplomat is beyond training, as it depends on human nature in all its diversity. The establishment of the *Académie politique* by Colbert de Torcy in 1712, was an explicit recognition of diplomacy as a separate profession, a fact that was strongly emphasized by Callières. The Academy's curriculum included practical knowledge, particularly of negotiation, instruction in languages, and the interpretation of treaties.[9] The foundation of the Regius Chairs of History at Oxford and Cambridge in 1724, intended for the training of diplomats, proved ultimately to be an academic affair rather than a diplomatic one. An entrance examination to the diplomatic service was introduced in 1856. The British Foreign Office adapted itself also to the political and international changes taking place at the beginning of the twentieth century, as well as following the end of the two world wars.[10]

Examinations for entry into the American diplomatic service were introduced in 1924 with the Rogers Act, which established the professional foreign service of the State Department. The first class of American diplomats entered the foreign service school in 1925, alongside an attempt to convince Congress that tenured diplomats would be preferable to political appointees.[11]

Foreign ministries use various methods to school diplomats, alternating between different skills and knowledge. The United States foreign service teaches about eighty languages, and aspiring diplomats now have to acquire some expertise on various subjects—humanitarian affairs, the environment, narcotics, trade, and finance. But, apparently, no agreement could be reached regarding the essential qualities of diplomats—their character, natural intelligence, and temperament.[12]

The schooling circuit in departments and the very first assignment of a diplomat constituted the best apprenticeship for the old guard of British diplomats in the first part of the twentieth century. The pattern was quite obvious. Almost everyone spent some time abroad in the capitals of the continental powers, sharpening their linguistic knowledge, as proficiency in French and German was a primary requisite for a diplomat. Despite probable dullness and boredom, the first posts at the lower ranks were the training grounds for some of the most successful British diplomats.[13]

In countries with less established foreign services, the beginning of a diplomatic career was decided by favoritism, and occasionally in dubious circumstances. When the Chilean Pablo Neruda arrived in Rangoon in October 1927, he was bewildered by the logistical arrangements and the loneliness of a "terrible exile." When he moved to Ceylon "his only companions were a dog, a tamed mongoose and a servant."[14]

In the case of Joseph Grew, it was the longing for the sea and distant travel that attracted him to a diplomatic career, in what was considered to be an uncharted course. While touring France, he received a telegram from an acquaintance that the vice consul in Cairo was looking for a private secretary. He telegraphed back, despite his parents' displeasure, "Accept unconditionally."[15]

George Kennan was surprised to be accepted into the diplomatic service. His oral examination was headed by Grew. He began his service in 1926, and in 1934 he was assigned to the Moscow Embassy. For choosing the diplomatic service, he wrote in his memoirs: "it was the first and last sensible decision I was ever deliberately to make about my occupation."[16] Charles Bohlen was introduced by his uncle to a high-ranking officer at the State Department before taking the examinations. He came to his oral examination smelling of bootleg gin, in violation of the Prohibition Law, and again it was his uncle who saved him. After four months at the foreign service school, he was sent to Prague in 1929, as a vice consul. Undoubtedly, entry to the diplomatic service in our time is less colorful. At the end of a long career Ivone Kirkpatrick has reached the true, though banal conclusion, that "in diplomacy, as in every other enterprise, luck seems to run in cycles."[17]

As far as diplomatic appointments are concerned, the diplomat inhabits a dual world: one at home and the second global in its reach, with capital cities signaling either reward or punishment. The structure of the diplomatic service makes the dispersal of rivals and newcomers a procedure played according to the rules of the game. Seniority is of importance in diplomatic rituals and promotions, and resistance is rare. When Lord Bertie, the ambassador in Paris, insisted that Nevile Henderson had to be transferred to Athens, Henderson strongly objected and was willing, in protest, to enlist in the army. The Foreign Office found someone else to take his place in Athens. He remained in Paris for four more years, but was not invited to Lord Bertie's house for at least a year.[18]

The ups and downs of diplomacy gravely damaged Harold Nicolson's career. When he was posted to Teheran he felt that he had been forced to leave for exile as a result of manipulation and scheming. Later on his position became shaky at the Foreign Office. He had been demoted to the rank of first secretary before being posted to Berlin, his last diplomatic assignment. Ultimately, he decided to leave the diplomatic service. Reading his diary, it is evident that he regretted his departure from the Foreign Office. When he was invited for lunch at the German Embassy in Rome in January 1932, he grew nostalgic for the diplomatic climate: "so calm, so quiet, so distinguished." An entry in August 1935 is most revealing. "I dreamt that Vansittart wrote and asked me to join the Foreign

Office again. My disappointment when I wake up and found that this was only a dream . . ."[19]

Gentlemanly manners are now a matter of the past. Appointments and promotions are regulated according to orderly rules. The State Department restricts the amount of time that can be spent in the service without promotion. Political appointments, however, remain widespread, with a negative impact on professional diplomats. Since the early 1960s, the ratio of career diplomats to political appointees in the United States is about two to one.[20]

—— ••• ——

Women have cast their shadow on the diplomatic profession for a long time. The appointment of women to diplomatic assignments began to be considered seriously only in the period between the two world wars. In the United States, Joseph Grew, the chairman of the foreign service personnel board, devised various tactics for excluding women. He feared that they would ruin the morals at the State Department. Privately, he recommended that the department should fail women in their oral examinations, on the grounds that they did not possess the necessary qualifications. There were other grounds of prejudice—the supposed inability of women to keep secrets, and the fear that the social life in missions abroad would be disrupted.[21] The breakthrough came gradually after the nomination of President Franklin Roosevelt. By 1953 there were forty-three women in the foreign service. During the sixties recruiting policy was made identical for both women and men. As of 2005, more than a third of foreign service officers are women.[22]

In 1889, the first "lady type writer" was appointed in the British Foreign Office. In the Second World War, a white paper stated that the admission of women to the administrative grades would be considered. The first female diplomats on a permanent basis were appointed in the late forties. In 1987, Veronica Sutherland was the first married woman to serve as ambassador to Abidjan. By 1994, women formed 28 percent of the British diplomatic service. In Norway, where only one woman was listed in 1918, 50 percent of the employees of the foreign ministry are women, though they constitute only one-third of the diplomats.[23]

For the first women who gained entry to the diplomatic service this involved surmounting a high barrier. President Franklin Roosevelt appointed Ruth Bryan Owen, the eldest daughter of Woodrow Wilson's first Secretary of State, as a minister to Denmark. After her marriage to a Dane, and despite her popularity, she was obliged to leave the service. Frances Willis was nominated in 1953 as the first woman to serve as a chief of mission, although she had passed the foreign service examinations in 1927. Willis, who remained single, complained of discrimination only after her retirement: "it takes long, hard work to break down the prejudice."[24]

——— •◆• ———

It would be correct to say that a diplomatic career "has unpredictable content in a predictable form." It calls for a life spent abroad, frequent transfers, difficulty in reconciling family obligations, and the futility of a large part of the diplomatic rituals. David Kelly mused on the lapse "into servitude in return for security"; but George Kennan, despite all the disappointments, concluded his memoirs with a sense of accomplishment and elation at having been a diplomat, adding that: "diplomacy, as a career, is tragic only in its results, not normally in its experiences."[25]

For centuries the reputation of diplomats suffered from what was presumed to be their privileged and luxurious way of life. The reality of the diplomatic occupation, as it unfolds publicly and privately, at home and abroad, does not necessarily correspond to that image. Diplomats' style of life and the exclusive setting of their vocation, oblige them to engage in a Sisyphean struggle to bridge the gap between the presumed indulgencies of their lives and the false image associated with their profession. The privileges granted to diplomats were closely intertwined with the traditions of court society. Envoys were elevated to a distinctive class of practitioners as a result of being close to power. Legislation on the excessive expenses of ambassadors had already preoccupied the Venetian Senate. The introduction of popular sovereignty at the end of the eighteenth century opened the way for the battle over diplomatic privileges.[26]

The exclusiveness of diplomatic life is still preserved and sanctified by international law. Diplomatic memoirs are peppered with descriptions of a lavish style of life—limousines, uniformed chauffeurs, diplomats' families attended by an army of servants, and banquets beneath candelabras of Bohemian crystal. In a letter to his daughter from Yalta, Piers Dixon presented the other side of the coin: "the whole business puts considerable strain on the brain and digestion. The difficulty as always at these gatherings is to get enough sleep and exercise."[27] There is, of course, the undeniable abuse of diplomatic privileges and immunity, which extends from smuggling and violation of parking rules to the criminal support of international terrorism. A luxurious way of life, however, is hardly the norm for the majority of contemporary diplomats, and is in any case balanced by the travails and risks of the diplomatic career.[28]

Diplomats live in a world of their own, in the isolation and social intensity of embassy life. The character and competence of the head of mission is, in this case, of critical importance. While diplomatic routine tends to be boring, the measure of rapport and informal relations among colleagues may prove to be either rewarding or punishing. There is an overlap between the private and the public spheres, as diplomats continue to carry out their obligations even during receptions, balls, and occasional meetings. Stamina and energy are as necessary as a balanced temperament in order to resist temptation and exhibit empathy toward foreigners without "going native."[29]

Wives did not accompany their husbands in embassies until the eighteenth century. Lady Mary Wortley Montague was the first British wife to accompany her husband, who was ambassador to Constantinople in 1716. Spouses are important members of any diplomatic entourage, but also a potential cause of strain. Katie Hickman provides a vivid and comprehensive perspective on being the companion of a professional diplomat—the loneliness, the dependency, and the yearning for contact with home. The fanfares tend to fade swiftly, but the ceremonies and receptions remain exhausting for most women, followed by the return home with its asymmetry in status and the standard of living.[30]

In recent years the diplomat's spouse has emerged as an autonomous individual. There is explicit recognition in Western foreign ministries of the spouse as playing a valuable role in the diplomat's affairs. Foreign services are now more forthcoming in providing support for spouses who wish to pursue their own careers.[31]

— •◦• —

The life of the diplomat is nomadic, full of farewells and a spirit of nostalgia. Pablo Neruda referred to it as a "luminous solitude."[32] The diplomatic career is divided in accordance with different landscapes and climates, other cultures and ways of life, and, occasionally, the demands of hostile regimes. Callières maintained that diplomats should continue to travel at an advanced age, when they were capable of reflection. Piers Dixon wrote in his diary: "I feel that my life lacks necessary constructive thread." And as for diplomacy, it is "necessary perhaps in the modern complicated structure of society, but not all-absorbing, not really constructive. It is a series of improvisations, calling for durable intellectual qualities."[33]

Indeed, not a few diplomats view with horror the last years of their career. Ivone Kirkpatrick saw retirement "rather as dying."[34] Even the most distinguished diplomats may retire embittered and frustrated. Satow retired well before the statutory age of retirement, pessimistic about his chance of influencing policy in the Foreign Office. Rumbold was disappointed at not being offered an appropriate nondiplomatic post, and for not receiving a peerage. George Kennan retired twice, the first time in the early fifties, against his wish.[35] George Rendel provides consolation for an occupation that rarely is complimented in public for its achievements: "A man may waste practically his whole life in it, and have nothing to show except a few minor social assets and recollections. . . . but one successful achievement may more than justify the work of a lifetime."[36]

Diplomacy is a hazardous profession. It could be said that diplomats serve at their own risk. In no other period of history since the seventeenth century has the safety of diplomats been so precarious. In the first part of the twentieth century, the outbreak of war exposed diplomats to risk and inconvenience. Kennan was confined under armed guard by the Germans at the beginning of the Second World War. Lancelot Oliphant, the British ambassador in Brussels, was captured in 1940 and remained a prisoner for over a year.[37]

In recent decades the brutal murder of diplomats, and the disregard for the inviolability of envoys and their premises, has become a frequent occurrence. In the last decade alone, ten American diplomats have been assassinated. The embassies of the Unites States, Great Britain, and Israel resemble military compounds. Notorious instances of attacks on embassies were those on the American Embassy in Teheran in November 1979, the bombing of the Israeli embassy in Buenos-Aires, and the attack on the American Embassy in Nairobi. Some terrorist attacks are supported by sovereign governments.[38]

— •◦• —

Is, as is generally assumed, the diplomatic corps the natural milieu for diplomats? It is, after all, the preserved domain of its practitioners. But the corps is illusive in structure, constantly changing according to the nomadic migration of envoys, and operating in an almost completely voluntary manner. The diplomatic corps maintains the formal equality of states, and is, perhaps, the embodiment of diplomatic culture.[39] But, to fully understand diplomats' role within it, we must take into consideration their divided loyalties—their solidarity with their colleagues, the interests of their country, and their own diplomatic convictions.

The duality of the formal and ceremonial, on the one hand, and the informal and social, on the other, is central to the corps. Since its early beginning in the fifteenth century, the corps has emerged as a diplomatic body comprised entirely of ambassadors and envoys residing in the same capital[40]—albeit assembling in a certain place in a random way. Vita Sackville-West, always sarcastic about diplomacy, remarked that the corps was a collection of people thrown together "through a purely fortuitous circumstance, with nothing in common except the place we happen to find ourselves in."[41]

Hovering above the corps is the doyen, the ambassador who delivered his credentials at the earliest date. He is only the first among equals, and his position and status rest on personal traits rather than any formal authority. Doyens are not independent actors, and should obtain the approval of their colleagues before acting on their behalf, usually in matters of prerogatives and privileges. They may, however, be highly instrumental in preserving the cohesion of the diplomatic corps, and in advising as regards joint action.[42]

The extent to which diplomats invest in coordinating their actions with colleagues, beyond courtesy calls, remains debatable. But the informal exchange of opinions is common. In his dispatches from Berlin, Horace Rumbold mentioned having compared notes with the French and American ambassadors and others of his colleagues. And at dinners and receptions information is gathered openly.[43] The probability that the corps will act on a unified basis is quite limited. *Démarches* are likely to occur in the capitals of authoritarian regimes, or when a member of the corps is faced with an unacceptable violation of privileges. The corps, nonetheless, has the potential for taking initiatives beyond routine and protocol. In the past it has acted as a multipolar broker, guiding new regimes into membership in the international society and providing a collective judgment on the resolution of a particular crisis.[44]

Solidarity among diplomats is no longer based on aristocratic origins,[45] though the diplomatic corps remains a distinct group with its traditions and norms. It is a diplomatic community with similar experiences and a common professional code. The duality of closeness and remoteness is inherent to the diplomatic corps. In guarding the interests of their country, diplomats remain lone wolves; but for the common good to be preserved they must adhere to the universal standards of international society.[46]

7

—— •◦• ——

The Courtiers of Civilization

THE PORTRAYAL of the professional diplomat in Western civilization is rather ambiguous, of dubious accuracy, and ultimately testifies to flagrant ingratitude. Diplomats' predicament is particularly apparent in their clash with rulers and warriors, where it is revealed that they are, after all, victims of their vocation's call. Ambassadors will continue to be absent from neoclassical pedestals; only the glimpses of past glamour will still shine.

In fact, the good diplomat is the courtier of civilization by being a symbol of peace, a custodian of public virtues, and the flag bearer of the practices of a functional and civilized international society. Thus, the mission of the diplomat is both tragic and epiphanic, and with no safe bounds. *Ambactiare*, to go on a mission, is the primary and fundamental meaning of diplomatic destiny. The circumstances and substance of a diplomatic mission change from time to time, but, regrettably, this does not apply to the reputation of the diplomat.

The diplomat has survived the trials and traps of modernity, but has not advanced much beyond the fate of the Renaissance envoy, namely, to uphold his or her country's interests, "aided by no more than his own wit, courage and eloquence."[1] The diplomat's reputation is structured by real causes, but no less, by implicit rumors and disguised insinuations. Jules Cambon has rightly commented that diplomats are not "the spoilt child of history."[2]

The dim view taken of diplomats' profiles is striking in comparison with the heroic posture in which statesmen, rulers, and captains of war like to portray themselves, particularly, since most crises in international relations are of their making. Diplomats somehow managed to avoid a coherent definition of their character and socioeconomic status. By now their privileges are not attached to a specific social class; and they have remained one of the king's men, while other public servants converted themselves into being the representatives of the "people" as well. As historical actors, diplomats have assumed many personae—honorable spies, strangers, shadowy agents, courtiers who serve their countries and kings, as well as timid appeasers and dull bureaucrats. Apparently, their characters are no longer synchronized with the swift pace of modern life. The diplomats' cautious and reasonable rhetoric and prudent pleading run against the popular temperament, as they perform for audiences who prefer clear-cut statements. The diplomatic golden rule would seem to have proved to be too abstract and too elusive.

From the very beginning, the diplomatic character was imbued with dubious dualities. Sir Henry Wotton's aphorism, perhaps the most quoted in the history of diplomacy, has been elevated to embody the epitome of the diplomatic craft, despite its origins in a misunderstanding.[3] While the description of the ambassador as "an honest man, sent to lie for the good of his country" corresponds well with the charm and duplicity of Hermes, the messenger of the gods, it does not fit the accusation that diplomats are timid and inept. But when the image of the diplomat as an honorable spy was in decline, the great revolutions of the eighteenth century gave rise to new and more devastating accusations against diplomats. For the continental revolutionaries, as well as for the American proponents of a "new diplomacy," diplomats were the agents of the old regime, messengers of an international order infested with entanglements and machinations.[4] The gravest accusation leveled against diplomatic envoys was that diplomacy itself is inherently corrupt, and by implication also futile and unnecessary.

Diplomats became easy prey for the hunt. They were victims of their vocation, since the practice of diplomacy calls on them to be ambiguous and moderate, and to suppress the truth when necessary. Diplomats were blamed first for the outbreak of the First World War, because of their secretiveness and intrigues, and then for devising the policy of appeasement. With the emergence of the Cold War era new theories and strategies of threats and signals were assumed to be more effective than ordinary diplomatic channels. Last, diplomats were influenced by political trends, as described by Eban and Kennan: "domestic opinion is liable to make the diplomat the scapegoat for the nation's inability to get its own way."[5]

— •◦• —

In the one place where diplomats could have found refuge—literature— they are often vilified and ridiculed. Writers, from Anthony Trollop to

Graham Greene, have inflicted a lasting damage on the reputation of diplomacy. And the list is a long one, including George Sand, Balzac, Proust, Mark Twain, Henry James, and Somerset Maugham.[6] Diplomats appear in Tolstoy's *Anna Karenina* in the least important episodes, as frivolous, uprooted men, with no real substance. Vrónsky, Anna's lover, was obliged by his reckless behavior and need to escape unwarranted traps to repeatedly deploy all his "diplomatic talents." In another episode, at Princess Betsy's salon, an ambassador's wife is sitting next to an attaché, both embarrassingly, are at a loss as to what to talk about, though the diplomatist believes that "once one has a theme, it is easy to embroider on it." In a revealing scene, Lévine, Tolstoy's hero, is chatting to Lvov, the husband of Natalie, his wife's sister. Lvov, "a diplomat who had passed all his life in the capitals abroad, where he had been educated," returns home, not because of unpleasantness, but for the sake of his children's education. Though, a likable person, he is cast as an uprooted man, far from what is dear to Tolstoy—redemption, the people, and the return to the Land.[7]

Orlando by Virginia Woolf, is a burlesque written "half in a mock style" about a diplomat serving in Constantinople, "properly scented, curled and anointed," but utterly depressed by diplomatic ceremonies and his mission. Orlando's adventures are replete with grotesque occurrences, among them his change of sex. Both Virginia Woolf and Vita Sackville-West, to whom the book is dedicated, detested diplomacy, and pleaded with Harold Nicolson, Vita's husband, to leave his diplomatic career altogether. Among other complaints, the need to serve as a hostess in diplomatic events, made Vita "shiver."[8]

It is better not to incur an artist's wrath. James Joyce, who sought Horace Rumbold's support in connection with his theatrical work, was so incensed when Rumbold, in his capacity as the head of the delegation at Berne, did not answer his letter, that he changed the name of the English barber in *Ulysses* from Billington to Rumbold. When Joyce heard of Rumbold's appointment as ambassador to Poland, he wrote a poem titled "The Right Man in the Wrong Place," in which Rumbold was "puffed, powdered and curled."[9] Mention may also be made of Pablo Neruda, who lived in a world not regularly frequented by other diplomats. His appointments and amorous affairs advanced, first and foremost, according to political and poetical rhythms, though not necessarily to diplomatic ones.

— •• —

Diplomats are particularly vulnerable in their clash with sovereigns, where the aura of privilege and proximity to power often prove to be a double-edged sword. In the extreme case of a struggle between a virtuous prince and an ideal diplomat, the latter is merely a hunter with feeble arrows, or in Machiavellian terms, a fox of the second order. The diplomat is almost inevitably the civil servant chosen, by his manners, image, and practices, to serve as a scapegoat.

Diplomats act, mostly, through channels that are concealed from the public eye, while heads of state and military men dominate the stage of great gestures. Diplomats tend to leave as little as possible to *fortuna*, and refrain from practices associated with such concepts as "national honour," or "national destiny." At more than one junction of history, diplomats have been faced with a cruel dilemma: to tell the truth for the sake of their nation and fellow countrymen, or to remain loyal to rulers and politicians. And with truth, comes retribution.[10]

It is one of the ironies of history that in the past diplomats were given considerably more discretion in conducting the state's affairs, when they were subordinate to their sovereign. Nevertheless, mutual mistrust and the absence of clear instructions often clouded the relationship between envoys and their masters. Rulers are not necessarily courageous and diplomats are not necessarily timid, nor do heads of state comprehend the call of the moment better than their envoys. Referring to the great diplomats of the nineteenth century, A. J. P. Taylor writes that they were dependent throughout most of their careers on less-talented and slow-witted monarchs; adding that many diplomats, though vain or stupid, "had something like a common aim—to preserve the peace of Europe without engendering the interests or security of their countries."[11]

Diplomats and politicians have a long list of grievances, against one another. Heads of state demand that diplomats be faithful and crafty, but tend to ignore, or even punish those who stray beyond the bounds of their orders. Diplomats blame politicians for their irresponsible rhetoric, and for compromising national interests for the sake of domestic political gains. While politicians and military men can never resist scoring a point, they require that diplomats perform the thankless task of national apologia.[12]

Statesmen as well as warriors act within the "internal lines" of the domestic and the external, and have constituencies. The diplomat may serve grand designs, but is rarely in a position to gather the harvest openly, and is excluded for good reasons from any hero worship. The creed of diplomats is obedience; they seek to cope not conquer. Politicians act more according to their will, and, whenever expedient, tend to bypass or ignore diplomats. Diplomats are called to display self-control, and conceal their reservations; their repertoire is that of caution, guardedness, and suspended judgment. Nicolson stated candidly that "the impassivity which characterizes the ideal diplomatist must render him much disliked by his friends."[13]

Evidently, diplomats were performing against the *mentalité* of the modern age. They were men of the status quo, when change was the order of the day, and prudence was miscast as appeasement. It is no accident that the foremost writers on diplomacy advised diplomats to tread a safe path in their relations with sovereigns; to avoid disputes, and never to be seen wiser or more learned, as there was more to be regretted from words than from silence. Machiavelli, who complained that he was undeservedly afflicted by the malice of fortune, counseled envoys to study the prince and the men surrounding him carefully, before discharging their functions. He further recommended that, "good policy, whoever suggests it, comes from the wisdom of the Prince."[14]

De Vera, Gentilli, and Wicquefort, all stressed the importance of obedience to the prince.[15] Callières dwelt at length on the relationship between an envoy and his sovereign. He had a reserved appreciation of princes, but called on diplomats to be respectful, not to take credit for advices given, and to be exact in their promises. The diplomat should "put himself in the place of a prince," in order to correctly judge the situation, and to praise him whenever suitable. Callières himself was careful to publish his treatise on diplomacy only after the death of Louis XIV.[16]

History has vindicated the caution and carefulness of diplomats in dealing with their superiors. Richelieu, who was shrewd and tactful in his relations with Louis XIII, complained of being the most wretched of men in France. The King disliked him personally, and the innumerable plots to remove him from office never abated.[17] Louis XIV took a personal interest in diplomacy, carefully scrutinizing the activity of French diplomats, but ignoring them when he conducted secret negotiations. Napoleon called Talleyrand a "shit in a silk stocking." But after the defeat of the Emperor, it was left to him to bring France back to the negotiating table at the Congress of Vienna, and begin the restoration of its stand in European diplomacy.[18]

— ·•· —

For many years the British Foreign Office was the symbol of lack of foresight and inefficiency. Palmerston was known for his derogatory remarks directed at diplomats.[19] At the beginning of the twentieth century, political interference in diplomatic affairs increased, intensifying during Lloyd George's premiership. After the First World War, it became the prevalent pattern. In addition, diplomats had to cope with the involvement of royal appointments, those of King Edward VII, in particular. In the autocratic regimes of Russia and Germany, where monarchs played a central political role, the plight of diplomats was even worse.

Lloyd George was notorious for ignoring professional diplomats. He opposed having only members of the Foreign Office and the diplomatic service accompanying him to the peace conference. He managed to upset Curzon by preferring to take his secretary, Vansittart, to accompany him in his meeting with Briand, the French Foreign Minister. Nicolson, while insisting on the distinction between diplomacy and foreign policy, and on the importance of political guidance, was full of contempt for the "self-centred, ill informed, arrogant behaviour of world leaders" at Versailles. He was, on the other hand, full of admiration for Eyre Crowe, Robert Vansittart, and Horace Rumbold—the diplomats.[20] Sir Eyre Crowe was denied the permanent undersecretaryship, after a clash with Edward Grey, as he insisted on honoring Britain's commitment to France in the event of a German attack. Crowe found himself in agreement with Clemenceau at the Paris Peace Conference, a collaboration that was also enhanced by cultural affinity.[21]

Neville Chamberlain declined to be accompanied by any Foreign Office official at the Munich Conference. Nevile Henderson's *Failure of a Mission* is an apologia for a lost mission, but he was right to comment that "An ambassador is a public servant, and as such does many things which may be distasteful to him as a private individual." In this particular case, statesmen, and diplomats were playing according to the rules, when such rules had already been abandoned.[22]

On the other side of the diplomatic spectrum stands the imposing personality of Robert Vansittart, characterized by his biographer, Norman Rose, as a "quintessential outsider." As the permanent undersecretary, he strongly opposed the policy of appeasement. Vansittart declined Eden's offer of the Paris Embassy, and was later abruptly removed from his office by Chamberlain. He was elevated to the post of chief diplomatic adviser to the government, but became utterly isolated.[23] Winston Churchill tended to use vacancies abroad as a political expedient. He offered the Washington Embassy to Halifax, despite the latter's dislike of the United States, in order to make way for Eden. Churchill was not content to follow, in any case, what he dubbed as the subtotal of diplomatic fears.[24]

—— •◆• ——

The plight of diplomats across the Atlantic was no better, perhaps even worse. Washington's farewell address, drafted by Thomas Jefferson and

Alexander Hamilton, did not augur well for the beginnings of American diplomacy. Jefferson was explicit in his contempt of professional diplomats. And diplomacy did not occupy a great deal of Lincoln's time. Eugene Schuyler was the first American diplomat to be trained professionally. During his career he severely criticized the secretary of state, Elihue Washburne, who later on, assisted by his friends in the Senate, managed to block his nomination to the post of assistant secretary of state.[25]

Theodore Roosevelt has given a blunt account of the cruel reality of American diplomacy at the beginning of the twentieth century. In a letter to Joseph Grew he wrote: "I have put you in the service because I believe in you, but I can't recommend it as a permanent career. There is no career; it's all politics. I will keep you there as long as I am president but my successor will in all probability throw you out to make way for political henchmen, and then where will you go?"[26] American diplomats served, after all, as personal envoys of the president. Dean Acheson confided that all presidents he had known had doubts about the State Department, but demanded absolute loyalty. Averell Harriman testified in 1963 that the career of diplomats was ruined by having the right views at the wrong time.[27] Kissinger's memoirs are most revealing in this regard. He complimented the State Department's officers for being loyal, hardworking, and intelligent, but was convinced that there was a need to curtail the influence of the parochial bureaucracy. Diplomats can act successfully only if there is a "strong hand at the helm."[28]

Franklin Roosevelt had a deep mistrust of diplomats, apart perhaps from his fellow graduates of Groton and Harvard.[29] He deliberately ignored the State Department and bypassed Cordell Hull, despite Hull's influence in the Congress. Roosevelt was his own secretary of state, particularly on matters of war and peace.[30]

A generation later, the low esteem for the State Department had not changed. Both President John Kennedy and his brother Robert were known for their scathing criticism of professional diplomats. They regarded career envoys as timid, weak, and spineless. Kennedy chose Dean Rusk as a secretary of state, with the clear intention that he "would be a sort of faceless, faithful bureaucrat who would serve rather than attempt to lead," but soon came to regret his appointment. Kennedy also ignored and humiliated his ambassador to the United Nations, the revered leader of the Democratic Party, Adlai Stevenson.[31] Richard Nixon, Kennedy's archrival, showed no more respect for the State Department, intending on his nomination "to ruin the foreign service. I mean ruin it."[32]

George Kennan's career exemplifies the best in American diplomacy, but also some of its moments of embarrassment and humiliation. Kennan belongs to the short list of diplomats of the last century who had a true impact on world affairs.[33] His "long telegram" and the "X Article," were of exceptional influence on American policy, though in retrospect he came to regret that the term *containment* was elevated to the status of a doctrine.[34] Kennan was thoroughly humiliated when he was recalled back from Russia, after having been declared persona non grata. He learned from a newspaper of the appointment of Charles Bohlen as his successor in Moscow. Kennan was offered no new assignment by Dulles, and his colleagues and friends avoided him. He blamed the president and the secretary of state of being preoccupied with domestic politics. As a fellow Presbyterian, he did not find Dulles to be a pious man. His final conclusion in old age was that "Washington cannot tolerate for long any independent body of civil servants."[35]

During the years of McCarthyism, Kennan was personally involved in the scandalous case of John Patton Davies. Davies served in China on the staff of Gen. Joseph Stilwell in the years 1942–1944, and in 1949 and 1950 was attached to the policy planning staff, of which Kennan was the director. Davies was notable for his accurate reporting from China on the weakness of the Chinese Nationalists, compared with the competence of the Chinese Communists. Following the collapse of America's China policy, he was accused of being a pro-Chinese communist, and of holding left-wing views. Davies was subjected to a long series of investigations, and despite Kennan's efforts on his behalf, he was dismissed from the foreign service for "lack of judgement, discretion and reliability." Davies was never found guilty of any wrongdoing, and was fully rehabilitated only many years later.[36]

—— •◦• ——

A significant aspect of the diplomat's character derives from the fact that diplomacy is the craft of strangers. The diplomat, particularly in his role as a formal representative, embodies in his personality one of the prominent roles of Western civilization—that of the "other." The first diplomats appeared in history as strangers. Reciprocity made the diplomat sacrosanct, and expediency defined his probable lack of loyalty. As a historical actor the diplomat fulfilled many roles—whether false or true—that of the honorable spy, courtier and trader, as well as that of the timid appeaser and the dull bureaucrat. But the diplomat is not naturally associated with the notion of strangeness or otherness, or considered to be peripheral, living at the edge of society. On the contrary, the diplomat is part of the establishment and presumably close to power. Indeed, the stranger was always a source of both attraction and fear. Symbolically and geographically the diplomat is borderless person, or someone beyond the bounds of the familiar. But, as we will see, estrangement is inherent to the diplomatic craft, and being a stranger is both essential and beneficial to the diplomat.

There are three forms of estrangement that are relevant to diplomacy. The first defines diplomacy as the "mediation of estranged peoples, organized in states." The second is the estrangement inherent to the diplomatic exchange, and is beneficial to the accomplishment of the diplomat's mission.[37] The last is the estrangement of the diplomat from himself.

The essence of being a stranger was first brilliantly presented by Georg Simmel, and later complemented by Alfred Schuetz.[38] Simmel based his explanation on "the union of closeness and remoteness," as the stranger is both far and near, inside and outside, at the same time. The stranger is an objective observer of reality, because the stranger is not bound by roots to a certain place, nor by social ties that could prejudice his perception and assessment of the situation. Thus, the stranger's criteria for making judgments are often more general and more objective. Last, the stranger is perceived by others not as a private individual, but rather as representing "a certain type." It was Simmel's revelation that the state of being a stranger constitutes a specific form of social interaction. The diplomatic dialogue is a form of this kind, in which the parties recognize the distance between them, and view themselves as strangers who do not necessarily share the same interests, or the same world of meaning.[39]

Alfred Schuetz defined *strangeness* as a mechanism for objective interpretation. The stranger is forced to abandon his scheme of interpretation, and to acquire a new one in order to become oriented to the society he is approaching. In adopting new frames of reference, the stranger becomes an explorer beyond the boundaries of the familiar. Apart from this capability for objectivity, Schuetz also emphasized the stranger's doubtful loyalty.

It is, indeed, the task of the good diplomat as someone committed to true reporting, to objectively study other societies and the intentions of governments. For that purpose, as was mentioned earlier, diplomats should neither tie themselves to their chancery desks nor "go native."[40] Diplomacy requires a deliberate act of distancing and acknowledgment of the other as a stranger, as a prelude to dialogue. The diplomatic encounter is a setting where mutual trust is routinely displayed between strangers; social intimacy should not betray rivalry and divergent interests.

— ••• —

Diplomacy is an invitation to periodic exiles. The diplomat's nomadic life is defined by a simple form of estrangement. An inevitable consequence of the diplomat's mission is that he becomes a stranger. The diplomat's life is conducted behind barriers. As representative diplomats they are "extraordinary," their premises are "exterritorial," and their bodies, at least formally, are immune and untouchable.

Diplomats are strangers both in the societies of their placement, and in their own countries.[41] The return home of Averell Harriman and George Kennan was described by both in Odysseyan terms. Speaking to reporters Harriman remarked, "I primarily want to come back to my country . . . and I want to get to know this country again." Kennan wrote candidly, "now, for the first time, it fell to us to live in places that we owned."[42]

The perfection of the diplomatic code of behavior makes estrangement an immanent reality. Diplomats are called on to be in command of their tempers, and to distance themselves from every possible trap and distraction. More than any other writer on diplomacy Callières elaborated on this aspect of the diplomatic practice: "one must have calm, reservedness, a great deal of discretion, and patience in abundance."[43] In addition, diplomats usually desire to accomplish their diplomatic tasks without any sentimental involvement or intimacy that could impede their success as envoys of their country.

This pose of self-restraint, caution, and discipline has its price, the probability of not being true to oneself. This feeling of alienation intensifies when diplomats become aware that they are strangers not only when they are in the company of others, but also when they are alone. Self-estrangement is, perhaps, the highest price paid by diplomats for the sake of their countries. There is no apparent remedy for this diplomatic malady; each diplomat copes with it independently, as part of the struggle to preserve his or her inner self and individuality. A plausible venue for self-estrangement is the formation of an alternative identity by reflection, and by knowing oneself, *nosce te ipsum*. Simmel believed that by not having established ties, the stranger becomes a free person. Callières recommended that diplomats should occasionally forget their rank and entertain themselves in a free manner with their friends.[44] Thus, estrangement is not only a repression of the self, but also a path to emancipation, a mechanism for separating the private from the public life, part of diplomats' struggle to preserve their individuality. The most revealing in this regard is George Kennan: "I discovered that in this new role as representative . . . rather than just myself, the more personal idiosyncrasies and neuroses tended to leave me. . . . I welcomed with surprised relief the opportunity to assume a new personality behind which the old introverted one could retire, be relieved of some of its helplessness and even get some measure of perspective on itself."[45]

—— •◆• ——

The diplomat's conception of reality has its unique patterns. In one of the entries in his diary, Nicolson wrote: "I see both sides of every question. That is a mistake."[46] It is puzzling that Nicolson regarded the intellectual ability of diplomats to analyze a problem from all relevant angles as a personal weakness. Diplomats tend to relate to the prevalent, but have to imagine different possibilities and work for distant ends.[47] The diplomatic reality must be constructed in precise way, and based on careful observation of the possible. But the ability of diplomats to create a wide-ranging political conception is impeded by the materials with which they work. The multitude of cables, aide-mémoire, and protocols are fragments that are not sufficient for conceptualizing the broader perspectives of reality.[48] Thus, the dualistic approach of ambivalence and ambiguity is common to diplomatic practice. Suspended judgment is a preferable ploy, as it leaves options open, and provides time for consultation.[49] While diplomats are typecast as masters of changing settings, their ordinary inclination is toward maintaining the status quo and the *raison de système.*[50]

—— •◆• ——

Diplomats should be regarded as the courtiers of civilization by virtue of their ethics, and the substance of their practices. We posit, first, that there is inherent compatibility between the diplomat's ethics and practices. Second, that while he is occasionally depicted as a cynical pragmatist, walking in the fog of the "empire of circumstances," the good diplomat is, in fact, a crusader for the sake of truth. Diplomacy is a unique phenomenon in which morality does not necessarily negate practical considerations. It stems, first and foremost, from the nobility of diplomacy's ultimate goal—peace. The best diplomat cannot escape his moral obligation to advance the collective good by prudence and moderation. It should, however, be remembered that diplomacy is neither an intellectual endeavor nor a moral occupation; particularly since virtue is disclosed by performance, as well as the dependence of diplomats on their specific instructions. But, the convergence of such traits and faculties as prudence, loyalty, and honesty, which are necessary for the fulfillment of the diplomat's task, makes for moral behavior.[51]

All the great commentators on diplomacy have placed moral integrity at the forefront of the qualities that a successful diplomat must possess. Truthfulness is the only sound choice, even where the diplomat's own character is of a different inclination. Sir Henry Wotton's other advice to an aspiring diplomat was that "your truth will secure you." And Nicolson was fond of quoting the Latin epigram that "Others may, you may not" (*Aliis Licet, Tibi Non Licet*).[52] Deceit and duplicity are a short-lived ploy that is destructive to the diplomat's reputation, and undermines the essence of diplomacy. As the trustees of a civilized dialogue among nations, diplomats adhere to principles that are at the core of international ethics—prudence, trust, responsibility, and mutual accommodation. Fair judgment calls for an attempt to reconcile the desirable with the possible. The diplomat must consider what is advantageous and what is not, but also whether the end justifies the means.[53]

Diplomats act in the public domain and their credentials as an autonomous agent might be questionable. What validity does the diplomat's moral obligation hold, when measured against his or her country's policy? Whatever the diplomats' reservations, they have no choice but to faithfully execute their governments' instructions. Virtue and personal desire have, not once, to be sacrificed.[54] But, diplomats are not only practitioners who speak for the supreme source of power in their country, they are also human beings, citizens, and representatives of their nations and of civil society. Callières believed that the law of nations should never be violated, and that obedience to the prince had its bounds. Nicolson aimed toward a golden rule, "the gradual approximation of public to private morality." Though the moral supremacy of states is no longer acceptable, there is no satisfactory solution to Stanley Hoffman's reaffirmation that the rule of morality is not exactly the same between nations as it is between individuals, nor to Kennan's conclusion that despite the diplomat's moral impulses, his first obligation is to the national interest.[55]

The generally accepted truth is that diplomats rarely resign. In recent years only a handful of American and British diplomats have resigned in protest at their governments' policies in the Balkans and Iraq.[56] Absolute ideas are as a rule counterproductive in diplomacy. Gordon Craig and Alexander George were skeptical of moralists who are often "more concerned with the symbolic aspects of foreign policy than its actual substance."[57]

The case of diplomats who serve totalitarian regimes is certainly more complicated and clouded. The choice is usually extreme—either total subordination or resistance that subjects envoys to existential risk. Rudolf Nadolny, the German ambassador to Moscow, confronted Hitler personally on policy matters, and was dismissed or obliged to resign shortly afterward. Another ambassador to Moscow, Count Werner Friedrich von der Schulenburg, joined the resistance movement against Hitler, and might have been foreign minister if the plot against Hitler had succeeded. He was executed after the plot failed.

William Dodd, the American ambassador to Berlin, opposed appeasement and declined all invitations to attend Nazi rallies. But his successor, Hugh Wilson, praised Hitler and avoided criticism of German internal affairs. And in France, André François Poncet, who was considered to be the Führer's favorite, adjusted his positions according to circumstances, and served under the Vichy government. In contrast, Robert Coulondre and Alexis Saint-Léger, who strongly opposed France's policy toward Germany, paid personally for their stand. Coulondre was kept in the dark by his government, and Saint-Léger was dismissed from his post.[58]

It has now been authoritatively established by an independent committee of five historians that, contrary to its respectable reputation, the German foreign ministry committed collective sins under the Nazi regime.[59] German diplomats voluntarily served the Nazi Party, and assisted in implementing its policies. Many were members of the Nazi Party. The only ambassador to resign on ethical grounds was the German representative in Washington, Friedrich Wilhelm von Prittwitz.[60] On the opposite pole, diplomats risked their careers, and indeed their lives, in heroic efforts to save the lives of Jews in Continental Europe. Notable among them were Raoul Wallenberg of Sweden; Carl Lutz, the Swiss vice consul in Budapest; Chiune Sugihara, the Japanese consul in Kaunas; Abdol Hossein Sardari, Iran's representative in Paris; and Aristides de Sousa Mendes, the Portuguese consul in Bordeaux.[61]

The proposition that diplomats serves a moral purpose beyond the interests of their countries is usually met by skepticism.[62] It is true that diplomats who labor for the sake of peace also act on the basis of morally relativist terms—threats, coercive diplomacy, and military intervention. Permanent peace was, and remains, an elusive human ideal. But the descendents of Hermes are indeed the courtiers of civilization. They are the counselors and priests of peaceful relations; they hover above the conclusions of truces, ceasefires, and peace treaties. It is platitudinous to suggest that diplomats represent the best that is found in human nature. They are, however, the custodians of the idea of international society, and the guardians of international virtues.

Diplomacy constitutes intellectual property, granted for the sake of the public good. There is always a measure of nobility in the business of peace.[63] Diplomacy stands for *amicitia*, for a civilized and civilizing activity. It rests on the assumption that swords should be less potent, and that covenants should be upheld without the resort to force. It strives to conquer the middle ground in order to promote moderation, and construct paths of reason. Between solidarist perfection and realistic anarchy, the diplomat's natural inclination is toward the pluralist idea of international society. Diplomats' fates are bound up with the existence of rules and norms that make for a viable diplomatic culture.[64]

Callières advised diplomats not to confine their thoughts merely to their countries. The idea of the best diplomat has to be imagined anew, not in terms of different practices, but according to new purposes. To rise as a virtuous "proxenos," who has the legitimacy to also act for others. The ideal diplomat may follow a stoic path, already inherent to his craft, combining prudence, civility, a moderate temperament, and accommodation. Diplomacy is associated with conservative tendencies, while it is tied more to a cosmopolitan outlook than any other pursuit, as well as to the *civitas maxima* that might have been.[65]

8

— .•. —

Diplomacy Reconsidered

At the end of nineteenth century, the decline of diplomacy appeared as a theme that was ultimately never to leave the political discourse. Its persistence attests to diplomacy's ability, as an institution and an idea, to withstand the onslaught. Diplomacy has had many counselors of despair in modern times. They have presented its dysfunctions, the causes of its obsoleteness, and the case for its utter transformation. Disenchantment with diplomacy was one of the by-products of the Enlightenment. Revolutionaries of many kinds, whether genuine or false, demonstrated their contempt for diplomacy, among them French revolutionaries, Bolsheviks, liberal internationalists, and totalitarians of the extreme right. Another claim was that diplomacy had declined because mankind had abandoned God for materialism and secular humanism, opening the gates for a new barbarism. Diplomacy, it seems, was caught unarmed between the prophesies of a new dawn and the coming of the end of the world.[1]

The unsubstantiated accusations against the "old diplomacy," the ramifications of the policy of appeasement, and the secondary role allotted to diplomats during the Cold War era were all harmful to diplomacy's reputation. No less degrading was diplomacy's standing within international theory. Theorists are vociferous about its intellectual paucity, though they are unable to offer a meaningful analysis of its place in international politics. Theoretical models that had been refined into irrelevance, readily rejected diplomacy.[2]

An unfounded sense of intellectual inferiority is driving scholars to invent a new diplomatic theory. Diplomatic tradition and the majority of the literature in this regard, are considered to be a theory in a "narrow sense." Diplomacy is rich in its historical perspectives, practices, and sociological associations; it is futile and mistaken to abandon diplomatic tradition, only to be immersed in conceptual obscurity. The attempt to integrate diplomatic study with various theoretical approaches will inevitably lead to a new cul-de-sac. On the state of diplomacy one may concur with Lloyd George's perceptive remark: "It is a mistake to assume that the best are devoid of the worst and that the worst possess no trace of the best."[3]

Diplomacy is not an autonomous phenomenon, and its decline or rise is due to neither its intrinsic nature nor its practice. It is, rather, dependent on the structure of the world order, the prevailing international norms, and the quality of governance by the great powers. The euphoric days of 1989 and the "new world order" have passed, and to date the beginning of the twenty-first century is proving to be extremely unexpected. The collapse of international order, uncontrolled economic cycles, and the shift in the balance of power are beyond the diplomat's reach. His continuous presence and counsel may add stability and insight, when the complexity of international affairs is on the rise.

The increase in challenges confronting diplomats has accelerated since the First World War. The "new diplomacy" that was ushered in by the United States and Soviet Russia was shrouded in ambiguity and moral dualism from its very inception. A benevolent interpretation of Wilsonian internationalism is that it represented a return to the tradition of the Founding Fathers. In fact, the fourteen points contained nothing that contradicted the national interest of the United States. The Bolshevik Revolution exposed their expediency as a counterbalance to Soviet diplomacy before they were imposed on the European great powers.[4]

Open diplomacy was a path no one truly wanted to follow, other than the propagandist attempt by Leon Trotsky, the first foreign-policy commissar of the Soviet Union. According to the fourteen points, "diplomacy shall proceed always frankly and in the public view." This statement was too ambiguous to carry any real substance, but was enough to demoralize and scare veteran diplomats. The "new diplomacy" was "a blind alley for thought," in the words of Edward Grey. Indeed, "the vagaries of public opinion" exerted less influence on the status of diplomats than the reforms introduced by the foreign services of the great powers, and the growing tendency to centralize the conduct of foreign policy in the highest executive organs. But diplomacy was never the exclusive preserve of diplomats, and summits as well as conferences were neither an innovation nor a change in the essence of diplomacy.[5]

— .•. —

The challenges confronting diplomats are historically recurrent but critical nonetheless. Diplomats do not have to be confined to mainly consular labor, or restricted to being only one among the paraphernalia of "soft power," and be gradually banished from the political facets of diplomacy. The advance of NGOs, advocate associations, substate entities, and supranational actors to international affairs has created a crisis of representation that has not yet been solved. Both public and private diplomacy have created new settings but their merit is obscure. Neither political maneuvering nor human nature have changed, and the popular belief that "novelty and change are essential to validity and value" may well be mistaken.[6]

Public diplomacy was reinstated as a priority, largely in Western societies, fitting in well with the contemporary *zeitgeist*. Diplomats are not unaccustomed to public diplomacy if it means cultivating a favorable image for their country. It is a recognizable instrument of foreign policy that has changed only in its forms and techniques. Diplomats now attempt to compete in the open arena, and communicate directly with foreign audiences, though it may contradict the need to shield diplomacy from popular passions. One may call it the art of "engaging," but it is doubtful whether it is of significance for securing vital national interests; however, it certainly reflects discontent with contemporary international affairs.[7]

Public diplomacy is part of the tendency to be embedded in the new and ungovernable platforms of media inventions. New forms of communication and cyberdiplomacy have created a new dependency on the electronic environment. The new idol of virtual impressions is replacing contemplation and human judgment. Diplomats are adjusting themselves to new methods of communication, as diplomats have always done, though the information revolution is not enough to replace the diplomatic culture of their predecessors.

The WikiLeaks affair has exposed some of the risks involved in digital diplomacy. Julian Assange, the nomadic and anarchical founder of WikiLeaks, was convinced that total transparency was a cure for all public ills. A cache of a quarter of a million American diplomatic cables was made public. It was a flagrant demonstration of "open diplomacy." In "A Note to Readers" the *New York Times* wrote: "The Times believes that the documents serve an important public interest, illuminating the goals, successes, compromises and frustrations of American diplomacy in a way that other accounts cannot match."[8]

In fact, such a multitude of cables provides only a fragmentary and limited view of a much broader political reality. The disclosures of WikiLeaks did not change diplomatic relations, but exposed the risks involved in electronic communication, its methods of storage, and the rules of file sharing among bureaucracies. New measure of security and more discretion in diplomatic exchanges are to be expected. It is ironic, nonetheless, that in the past if a few documents, or even one significant letter, were leaked, this stirred up wide-ranging conflicts, but the leak of hundreds of thousands of documents may end in the banality of disclosure.

— ••• —

The most serious challenge to traditional diplomacy is the emergence of nonstate actors, constituting a development that goes far beyond multilateralism. It creates a new divide between professional diplomats and voluntary activists who exploit the political decay of Western civilization. There are also self-appointed citizen-diplomats as well as consultant agencies of former diplomats who serve various clients. The result is growing incoherence, and a more complex interplay of bargaining for all concerned. NGOs may be inventive in introducing issues that have been ignored by the international community but offer only an auxiliary venue at best. The activity of nonstate actors also involves a certain element of hubris, as they claim to represent a wide public or even mankind in general.

What public responsibility do nonstate actors have, to whom they are accountable, and for what common good are single-issue crusaders fighting for?[9] The drift toward inclusiveness must have its limits, otherwise we may witness a reversal to a new-medievalism of a plethora of entities, some with questionable credentials. Nonstate actors can neither replace nor reconstruct diplomacy.

— ••• —

Apart from distinguishing the informal dimensions of diplomacy, there is a tendency to ignore its formal aspects, which are still necessary for a viable and functioning international society. The field, we are told, is open to new actors. The current emphasis is on the voluntary emergence of social practices, not once dubiously defined as diplomatic, though open to different interpretations. There are theorists and diplomats who would consider the abolition of a separate cadre of diplomats altogether.[10] The disruption of professional diplomacy is considered to be an emancipatory act, while it is not far from the illusions of the "New Diplomacy" following the end of the First World War.

"Conditions of separateness" are not enough for the establishment of diplomatic relations.[11] Estrangement is conductive to the diplomatic encounter, but diplomacy itself does not exist in every condition of separateness. It is, indeed, premature to appraise the importance to diplomacy of the prospective plethora of polities, communities, social groups, and individuals. The inclusion of new masterless social agents with no evident forms of accountability is not encouraging.

The state, in fact, retains its privileged standing in world affairs, and continues to be the most influential actor in international society.[12] An "official" character, where diplomats are responsible to a political authority, is inherent to the diplomatic tradition. Evidently, no other actors acquired better skills than the professional diplomat in representing political entities, managing alliances, and influencing political views.

—— ·•· ——

Diplomacy was not invented a-priori as an abstract idea. It evolved out of necessity and through the refinement of its practices. The diplomat may have declined in power and prestige, but there is no substitute for his or her role as a resident envoy. Diplomacy remains most benevolent idea for the conduct of relations among political entities. In the complexity of international relations, the growing fragmentation of societies and continuing civilizational discontent, diplomats are needed more than ever. Diplomats, by the nature of their profession, are explorers of the common ground. They have a moral duty to guard public virtues, and to preserve the safety of all peoples.[13]

Diplomacy is encountering a process of "displacement" from the formal to the informal, from the state to various "relations" between social groups and individuals. The demystification of diplomacy dovetails with the marginalization of diplomats as enacted and executed by their masters. The revival of diplomacy is not attributed to its practitioners, but to its diversification into nonstate actors and social agents. Diplomacy, however, to be sustainable necessitates a political authority and a normative order, neither of which are guaranteed by this new "revival."

The future of diplomacy could be imagined only by the way the coming world order develops. It will thrive as long as states remain the salient form of international relations. Diplomacy developed at a slow pace, adapting itself to dramatic historical shifts, and changing structures and norms. The capacity for diplomatic innovation is often overestimated. If the past provides any clue to the future, progress by gradual measures and reform by adaptation will continue to prevail.

The thematic discourse of international affairs is changing, and there is a new scale of preferences, whether humanitarian, cultural, or commercial. However, expanding the diplomatic mission to encompass such topics as "chronic threats as hunger, disease and repression" also distracts from the principal goal of preserving peace by political means.

The solidarist approach will undoubtedly intensify the tension in the diplomat's role as practitioner and human being. The immediate transformation of the human condition is but an illusion. If a more reflective approach to diplomacy aspires to include NGOs and other nonstate actors in the diplomatic process, their place must be negotiated without discarding the existing diplomatic culture. Diplomacy neither should be localized nor domesticated. Diplomats should aim to preserve the "political" and the "international" as the essential part of their mission. And if diplomacy remains the instrument of governments, ambassadorial authority has to be restored.[14]

Diplomacy has been an integral part of the civilizational process, and it should remain so in any grand design for the advancement of the human condition. It has withstood many challenges simply because it offers the most reasonable way of conducting relations among nations. In this regard, Hedley Bull's forecast that diplomacy will continue "to flourish despite some elements of decline" is still valid.[15] Diplomacy has been a pillar of international politics for the last four centuries. If diplomats lose their prerogatives, international society will lose its best and most devoted messengers.

Notes

Chapter 1. Notes on the Origins and
Evolution of the Diplomatic Mission

1. Adam Watson, *Diplomacy: The Dialogue Between States* (New York: New Press, 1983), 18, 83, 92; also, Linda Frey and Marsha Frey, *The History of Diplomatic Immunity* (Columbus: Ohio State University Press, 1999), 108; James Der Derian, *On Diplomacy* (Oxford: Blackwell, 1987), 83. Der Derian is of the opinion that war is the womb in which politics and protodiplomacy develop.
2. Paul Sharp, *Diplomatic Theory of International Relations* (Cambridge, UK: Cambridge University Press, 2009), 10–19, 93–109; Harold Nicolson, *Diplomacy* (Oxford: Oxford University Press, 1963), 18; Der Derian, *On Diplomacy*, 6.
3. Ragnar Numelin, *The Beginnings of Diplomacy: A Sociological Study of Intertribal and International Relations* (London: Oxford University Press, and Copenhagen: Ejnar Munksgaard, 1950); Vinson Sutlive, Nathan Altshuler, and Mario Zamora(eds.), *Anthropological Diplomacy: Issues and Principles* (Williamsburg, VA: College of William and Mary, 1982).
4. Frey and Frey, *Diplomatic Immunity*, 3–14; Craig Barker, "The Theory and Practice of Diplomatic Law in the Renaissance and Classical Periods," *Diplomacy and Statecraft* 6 (1995): 595.
5. Raymond Cohen,"All in the Family: Ancient Near Eastern Diplomacy," *International Negotiation* 1 (1996): 11–28; Raymond Cohen, "The Great Tradition: The Spread of Diplomacy in the Ancient World," *Diplomacy and Statecraft* 12 (2001): 23–38; G. R. Berridge,

"Amarna Diplomacy: A Full-Fledged Diplomatic System?" in Raymond Cohen and Raymond Westbrook (eds.), *Amarna Diplomacy: The Beginnings of International Relations* (Baltimore: Johns Hopkins Press, 1999), 212–224. Berridge comes against the assertion that the Amarna archive permits us to claim that it provides uncontestable evidence of the existence of a sophisticated diplomacy; see also, Jeremy Black, *A History of Diplomacy* (London: Reaktion Books, 2010), 11–42. Black emphasizes the diplomacy of non-Western states.

6. Cohen and Westbrook, *Amarna Diplomacy*, 1–14; Joan Munn-Rankin, "Diplomacy in Western Asia in the Early Second Millennium B.C." in Christer Jönsson and Richard Langhorne (eds.), *Diplomacy* (London: Sage, 2004), vol. 2, 1–43; Bertrand Lafont, "International Relations in the Ancient Near East: The Birth of a Complete Diplomatic System," *Diplomacy and Statecraft* 12 (2001): 39–60; Pinhas Artzi, "The Diplomatic Service in Action: The Mittani File," in Cohen and Westbrook, *Amarna Diplomacy*, 205–211; Rodolfo Regionieri, "The Amarna Age: International Society in the Making," ibid., 42–53.

7. Raymond Cohen, "Reflections on the New Global Diplomacy: Statecraft from 2500 B.C. to 2000 A.D." in Jan Melissen (ed.), *Innovation in Diplomatic Practice* (Basingstoke, UK: Macmillan, 1999), 4; Lafont, "Ancient Near East," *Diplomacy and Statecraft* 12, 45–46; Mario Liverani, "The Great Powers Club," in Cohen and Westbrook, *Amarna Diplomacy*, 15–27.

8. Lafont, "Ancient Near East," *Diplomacy and Statecraft* 12: 42, 49.

9. Ibid., 44–45, 48–49. The duration of a stay in a foreign court could have lasted from a few days to up to several years or even twenty years.

10. Ada Bozeman, *Politics and Culture in International History: From the Ancient Near East to the Opening of the Modern Age* (New Brunswick and London: Prentice Hall, 1960), 118–149; Girija Mukerji, *Diplomacy: Theory and History* (New Delhi: Trimurti, 1973), 5–10; Frey and Frey, *Diplomatic Immunity*, 20–21; Kavalam Madh Panikkar, *The Principles and Practice of Diplomacy* (Bombay: Asia, 1956), 2–5.

11. Giri Deshingkar, "Strategic Thinking in Ancient India and China: Kautilya and Sunzi," in Jönsson and Langhorne, *Diplomacy*, vol. 2, 79–90.

12. T. N. Ramaswamy, (ed.), *Essentials of Indian Statecraft, Kautilya's Arthashastra for Contemporary Readers* (London: Asia, 1962); L. Rangarajan, "Classical Indian Diplomacy," paper, Conference on the 350th Anniversary of the Peace of Westphalia, Enschede, The Netherlands, July 1998.

13. Roswell Britton, "Chinese Interstate Intercourse Before 700 B.C.," in Jönsson and Langhorne, *Diplomacy*, vol. 2, 91–111; Mukerji, *Diplomacy*, 10–21; Frey and Frey, *Diplomatic Immunity*, 21–31.

14. Frank E. Adcock, and D. J. Mosley, *Diplomacy in Ancient Greece* (New York: Thomas and Hudson, 1975), 10, 15, 128, 177, 181; Martin Wight, *Systems of States* (Leicester: Leicester University Press, UK, 1977), 46–73; Andrew Wolpert, "The Genealogy of Diplomacy in Classical Greece," *Diplomacy and Statecraft* 12 (2001): 77–88; Keith Hamilton, and Richard Langhorne, *The Practice of Diplomacy* (London: Routledge, 1995), 8–10; Watson, *Diplomacy*, 86–89.

15. Adcock and Mosley, *Ancient Greece*, 152–154; Wolpert, "The Genealogy of Diplomacy," *Diplomacy and Statecraft* 12: 73–74.

16. Harold Nicolson, *The Evolution of Diplomatic Method* (London: Cassell, 1954), 3–14; Adcock and Mosley, *Ancient Greece*, 10, 155–71.

17. Wolpert, "The Genealogy of Diplomacy," *Diplomacy and Statecraft* 12: 76; Nicolson, *Diplomacy*, 19–23; Frey and Frey, *Diplomatic Immunity*, 14–15.

18. Adcock and Mosely, *Ancient Greece*, 160–161. Adcock considers the *proxenia* as the closest to some form of permanent representation; Wolpert, "The Genealogy of Diplomacy," *Diplomacy and Statecraft* 12: 74–76.

19. Watson, *Diplomacy*, 88; Adcock and Mosely, *Ancient Greece*, 161–165.

20. Brian Campbell, "Diplomacy in the Roman World (c. 500 B.C.–A.D. 235)," *Diplomacy and Statecraft* 12 (2001): 1–22; Nicolson, *Diplomatic Method*, 14–22; Bozeman, *Politics and Culture*, 204–211.

21. Frey and Frey, *Diplomatic Immunity*, 39–43, 51–52; Bozeman, *Politics and Culture*, 176–177.

22. Campbell, "The Roman World," *Diplomacy and Statecraft* 12: 8; José Calvert De Magalhães, *The Pure Concept of Diplomacy* (New York: Greenwood Press, 1988), 24–27; Nicolson, *Diplomatic Method*, 17–18. A refusal to accept a Roman delegation signaled an insult that necessitated redemption.

23. Frey and Frey, *Diplomatic Immunity*, 57; Nicolson, *Diplomatic Method*, 19.

24. Dimitri Obolensky, "The Principles and Methods of Byzantine Diplomacy," in Jönsson and Langhorne, *Diplomacy*, vol. 2, 112–129; Jonathan Shepard, "Information, Disinformation and Delay in Byzantine Diplomacy," in ibid., vol. 2, 130–174; Bozeman, *Politics and Culture*, 327–329, esp. 332.

25. Iver B. Neumann, "Sublime Diplomacy: Byzantine, Early Modern, Contemporary," *Millennium* 34 (2006), 865–888; Cohen, "Reflections," in Melissen, *Diplomatic Practice*, 12.

26. Shepard, "Information," in Jönsson and Langhorne, *Diplomacy*, vol. 2, 131–133; Bozeman, *Politics and Culture*, 329–332; Hamilton and Langhorne, *The Practice of Diplomacy*, 12–126; Nicolson, *Diplomatic Method*, 24–26.

27. Bozeman, *Politics and Culture*, 335–339 Frey and Frey, *Diplomatic Immunity*, 76–78.
28. Donald Queller, *Early Venetian Legislation on Ambassadors* (Geneva: Librairie Droz, 1966), 1; G. P. Cuttino, *English Medieval Diplomacy* (Bloomington: Indiana University Press, 1985); Garrett Mattingly, *Renaissance Diplomacy* (Harmondsworth, UK: Penguin, 1966), 15–31.
29. Donald Queller, "Medieval Diplomacy," in Jönsson and Langhorne, *Diplomacy*, vol. 2, 193–213; Queller, *Venetian Legislation*, 44, 50.
30. Mattingly, *Renaissance Diplomacy*, 32–35, 222–262; Queller, "Medieval Diplomacy," in Jönsson and Langhorne, *Diplomacy*, vol. 2, 207.
31. Matthews S. Anderson, *The Rise of Modern Diplomacy 1450–1919* (London: Longman, 1993), 36–38; Queller, *Venetian Legislation*, 50.
32. Mattingly, *Renaissance Diplomacy*, 26–28; Queller, "Medieval Diplomacy," in Jönsson and Langhorne, *Diplomacy*, vol. 2, 198–203.
33. Frey and Frey, *Diplomatic Immunity*, 83–108; Queller, "Medieval Diplomacy," in Jönsson and Langhorne, *Diplomacy*, vol. 2, 196–198.
34. Hamilton and Langhorne, *The Practice of Diplomacy*, 20–22; Queller, *Venetian Legislation*, 40; Frey and Frey, *Diplomatic Immunity*, 78–83; Queller, "Medieval Diplomacy," 193–194, 204–208. In the early fourteenth century, the number of Papal envoys was around forty-five. Apparently, Rome was the capital of the first diplomatic corps of Europe.
35. Bozeman, *Politics and Culture*, 458–468; Nicolson, *Diplomatic Method*, 27–30.
36. Bozeman, *Politics and Culture*, 464–468; Queller, *Venetian Legislation*, 14–16, 58. Queller has a more qualified estimation of Venetian diplomacy.
37. Mattingly, *Renaissance Diplomacy*, 109; Bozeman, *Politics and Culture*, 468–471.
38. Queller, *Venetian Legislation*, 28–43.
39. Wight, *Systems of States*, 53, 141; Fry and Fry, *Diplomatic Immunity*, 119–125; also Der Derian, *On Diplomacy*, 106.
40. Mattingly, *Renaissance Diplomacy*, 66–79; Nicolson, *Diplomatic Method*, 33.
41. Michael Mallett, "Italian Renaissance Diplomacy," *Diplomacy and Statecraft* 12 (2001), 61–70; Christian Reus-Smit, *The Moral Purpose of the State* (Princeton: Princeton University Press, 1999), 67–86; Hamilton and Langhorne, *The Practice of Diplomacy*, 29–35; Mattingly, *Renaissance Diplomacy*, 85–94.
42. Anderson, *Modern Diplomacy*, 2–11, 31–32, 46–48, 103–110; Hamilton and Langhorne, *The Practice of Diplomacy*, 35–40, 89–98, 110–115; Reus-Smit, *The Moral Purpose*, 87–121; Black, *A History of Diplomacy*, 11–118.

Chapter 2. Voices for Diplomacy:
Statesmen, Diplomats, and Philosophers

1. Also, Stuart Murray, "Consolidating the Gains Made in Diplomatic Studies: A Taxonomy," *International Studies Perspectives* 9 (2008), 22–39.

2. Headly Bull's definition is precise and complete: "The conduct of relations between states and other entities with standing in world politics by official agents and by peaceful means," Headly Bull, *The Anarchical Society* (London: Macmillan, 1982), 162–163. Bull wrongly dismisses Satow's definition: "Diplomacy is the application of intelligence and tact to the conduct of efficient relations between the governments of independent states," Ernest Satow, *A Guide to Diplomatic Practice* (London: Longman, Green and Co., 1922), vol. 1, 1. Scholars of the English school provide different definitions, though all take into consideration its importance to international society, Martin Wight, *Power Politics* 2nd ed. (Harmondsworth, UK: Penguin, 1986), 113, 117; Watson, *Diplomacy*, 11; Der Derian, *On Diplomacy*, 6; Sharp, *Diplomatic Theory*, 13; G. R., Berridge, *Diplomacy: Theory and Practice* (Houndmills, UK: Palgrave Macmillan, 2002), 1; Nicolson, *Diplomatic Method*, 14, 16; Nicolson, *Diplomacy*, 12–13; Ronald P. Barston, *Modern Diplomacy* (London: Longman, 1988), 1.

3. Harold Nicolson, *The Congress of Vienna* (London: Methuen, 1966), 164; Watson, *Diplomacy*, 223.

4. Abba Eban, *The New Diplomacy* (New York: Random House, 1983), 379; Barry Steiner, "Diplomacy and International Theory," *Review of International Studies* 30 (2004), 493; G. R. Berridge, Maurice Keens-Soper, and T. G. Otte, (eds.), *Diplomatic Theory from Machiavelli to Kissinger* (Basingstoke, UK: Palgrave, 2001), 107.

5. Also, Paul Sharp, *The English School, Herbert Butterfield and Diplomacy* (Clingendael: Netherlands Institute of International Relations, 2002), 12.

6. On *Advice to Raffaello Girolami When He Went as Ambassador to the Emperor*, see, Berridge, Keens-Soper, and Otte, *Diplomatic Theory*, 7–24.

7. Nicolo Machiavelli, *The Prince* (New York: Norton, 1977), 68.

8. G. R. Berridge, *Diplomatic Classics: Selected Texts from Commynes to Vattel* (Houndmills, UK: Palgrave, 2004), 20–30, 34–45.

9. François De Callières, *The Art of Diplomacy*, M. Keens-Soper and K. Schweizer (eds.) (Leicester, UK: Leicester University Press, New York: Holmes and Meier, 1983),69–70; Nicolson, *Diplomatic Method*, 50–53; Robert Knecht, *Richelieu* (London: Longman, 1991), 84–103, 218–220.

10. Berridge, *Diplomatic Classics*, 116; Berridge, Keens-Soper, and Otte, *Diplomatic Theory*, 31–82.

11. Antoine Pecquet (1700–1762) reversed in his treatise on diplomacy to Richelieu's emphasis on diplomacy. Pecquet elaborates on the different stages of negotiation, and on the importance of training, and the instruction given to diplomats. See, Hamilton and Langhorne, *The Practice of Diplomacy*, 70–71; Berridge, *Diplomatic Classics*, 160–170; Berridge, Keens-Soper, and Otte, *Diplomatic Theory*, 119–120.

12. Major works of Lipsius are *De Constantia* and *Politica*. De Vera drew heavily on Lipsius, and it seems that he influenced Grotius as well; Halvard Leira, "Justus Lipsius, Political Humanism and the Disciplining of Seventeenth Century Statecraft," *Review of International Study* 34 (2008): 669–692; Theodor Corbett, "The Cult of Lipsius: A Leading Source of Early Modern Spanish Statecraft," *Journal of History of Ideas* 36 (1975), 139–152.

13. Maurice Keens-Soper, "Abraham de Wicquefort and Diplomatic Theory," *Diplomacy and Statecraft* 8 (1997): 16–30; Berridge, *Diplomatic Classics*, 124–134; Hamilton and Langhorne, *The Practice of Diplomacy*, 68–69.

14. Berridge, Keens-Soper, and Otte, *Diplomatic Theory*, 5, 154.

15. Callières regarded Richelieu the model of a great statesman, *The Art of Diplomacy*, 69–70.

16. Ibid., 111, 168–169; also, Berridge, Keens-Soper, and Otte, *Diplomatic Theory*, 106–122; Hamilton and Langhorne, *The Practice of Diplomacy*, 68–71.

17. Callières, *The Art of Diplomacy*, 73.

18. T. G. Otte, "A Manual of Diplomacy: The Genesis of Satow's Guide to Diplomatic Practice," *Diplomacy and Statecraft* 13 (2002), 229–243; Berridge, Keens-Soper, and Otte, *Diplomatic Theory*, 125–144.

19. Satow, *A Guide*, vol. 1, 1.

20. Ibid., 145.

21. Nicolson, *Diplomacy*, 20.

22. Nicolson, *The Congress of Vienna*, 164.

23. Harold Nicolson, *Peacemaking, 1919* (London: Constable, 1933), 3–5, 207–209; Berridge, Keens-Soper, and Otte, *Diplomatic Theory*, 151–172.

24. Berridge, Keens-Soper, and Otte, *Diplomatic Theory*, 33–44.

25. Mattingly, *Renaissance Diplomacy*, 227–229, 273–274; Berridge, Keens-Soper, and Otte, *Diplomatic Theory*, 57–71.

26. Nicolson, *Diplomatic Method*, 48–50; Berridge, Keens-Soper, and Otte, *Diplomatic Theory*, 50–65; Headly Bull, Benedict Kingsbury, and Adam

Roberts (eds.), *Hugo Grotius and International Relations* (Oxford: Oxford University Press, 1992), 65–93, 95–131.

27. Berridge, Keens-Soper, and Otte, *Diplomatic Theory*, 176–179; Richard Davetak, "Discipline and Balance: Vattel and the Birth of International Relations Theory," paper, International Studies Association Convention, Washington, DC, February 1999; Herbert Butterfield, "The Balance of Power," in Herbert Butterfield, and Martin Wight (eds.), *Diplomatic Investigations* (London: George Allen and Unwin, 1966), 132; George MacDonald Ross, *Leibniz* (Oxford: Oxford University Press, 1984), 20–24, 112; Gottfried Wilhelm Leibniz, *Leibniz, Political Writings*, Patrick Riley, (ed.) (Cambridge, UK: Cambridge University Press, 1988), 121–145.

28. Martin Wight, *International Theory: The Three Traditions*, Gabriel Wight, and Brian Porter(eds.) (Leicester, UK: Leicester University Press, 1991), 154–159, 183–205.

29. Wight, *Power Politics*, 113–121; Robert Jackson, *Classical and Modern Thought on International Relations: From Anarchy to Cosmopolis* (New York: Palgrave Macmillan, 2005), 51–72; Herbert Butterfield, "The New Diplomacy and Historical Diplomacy," in Butterfield and Wight, *Diplomatic Investigations*, 181–192; Sharp, *The English School*; Der Derian, *On Diplomacy*, 88–96; Christer Jönsson and Martin Hall, *Essence of Diplomacy* (London: Palgrave Macmillan, 2005), 20; Andrew Hurrell, "Headly Bull and Diplomacy," paper presented at the International Studies Association Convention, New Orleans, March 2002; Geoffrey Wiseman, "Adam Watson and Diplomacy," Ibid.; Watson, *Diplomacy*, 14–21.

30. Costas M. Constantinou, *Human Diplomacy and Spirituality* (Clingendael: The Netherlands Institute of International Relations, 2006); Hoffman, John, "Reconstructing Diplomacy," *British Journal of Politics and International Relations* 5 (2003), 526.

31. Bozeman, *Politics and Culture*, 327, 465.

32. Sharp, *Diplomatic Theory*, 79–92; Jönsson and Hall, *Essence of Diplomacy*, 1–31; Edward Grey, *Twenty-Five Years, 1892–1916* (New York: F. A. Stokes, 1925), vol. 2, 277.

33. Nissan Oren, Statecraft and the Academic Intellectual," in Idem (ed.), *Intellectuals in Politics* (Jerusalem: The Magnes Press, 1984), 9–14; Murray, "Consolidating the Gains," *International Studies Perspective*, 9, 22–39.

34. Talleyrand remarked that "Metternich always lied but never deceived, Richelieu never lied but always deceived"; quoted in Victor Wellesley, *Diplomacy in Fetters* (London: Hutchinson, 1944), 213; Henry

Kissinger, *A World Restored* (Boston: Houghton Mifflin, 1957), 7–28, 41–61, 97–101; Nicolson, *The Congress of Vienna*, 38–44, 171; Taylor, A. J. P., *Europe: Grandeur and Decline* (Harmondsworth, UK: Penguin, 1967), 22–26.

35. Henry Kissinger, *Diplomacy* (New York: Simon and Schuster, 1994), 56–77; Kissinger, *A World Restored*, 20–40, 134–145; Nicolson, *The Congress of Vienna*, 141–157, 236–241. In comparison to the Continental statesmen, Castlereagh is praised in a more reserved way.

36. Nicolson, *Peacemaking 1919*, 50–73, 197–199; Kissinger's similar criticism of Gladstone, Kissinger, *Diplomacy*, 225–227, 230–232; Balfour has criticized Wilson's "Philosophy of Faith"; Felix Gilbert, *To the Farewell Address: The Beginning of American Foreign Policy* (New York: Harper and Row, 1965), 76–114. Many Americans looked on the prospect of participating in power politics with many reservations and hesitations.

37. Otto Bismarck, *The Man and the Statesman, Being the Reflections and Reminiscences of Otto, Prince von Bismarck* (London: Smith and Elder, 1898), vol. 1, 148–151, 238–249, 258–355; also, Henry Kissinger, "The White Revolutionary: Reflections on Bismarck," *Daedalus* 97 (1968), 906.

38. Ibid., 888–924; Kissinger, *Diplomacy*, 121–131.

39. Bismarck, *Reflections*, vol. 1, 223; A. J. P. Taylor, *Bismarck: The Man and the Statesman* (New York: Alfred A. Knopf, 1955), 115; Taylor, *Europe*, 87–90; Kissinger, *Daedalus*, 898.

40. Bismarck, *Reflections*, vol. 2, 244–245.

41. Henry, Kissinger, *The White House Years* (London: Weidenfeld and Nicolson, 1979), 26–268, 887. Nonetheless Kissinger has a full praise for the eminent diplomats of the Cold War era: George Kennan, Robert Lovett, John McCloy and Averell Harriman; Kissinger, *Diplomacy*, 463–466; also, Richard Wirtz, "Henry Kissinger's philosophy of International Relations," *Diplomacy and Statecraft* 2 (1991), 108–109.

42. Kissinger, *A World Restored*, 2.

43. Ibid., 54, 312–332.

44. John Gaddis, "Rescuing Choice from Circumstance: The Statecraft of Henry Kissinger," in Gordon A. Craig and Francis L. Loewenheim (eds.), *The Diplomats, 1939–1979* (Princeton: Princeton University Press, 1994), 564–592; Wirtz, "Kissinger," *Diplomacy and Statecraft* 2, 111.

45. Bull, *The Anarchical Society*, 182; Anderson, *Modern Diplomacy*, 26–27, 45–46.

46. Berridge, *Diplomatic Classics*, 124.

47. Mattingly, *Renaissance Diplomacy*, 37–38; Anderson, *Modern Diplomacy*, 45–46.
48. Quoted in Mattingly, *Renaissance Diplomacy*, 212; Montaigne, who lauded tranquillity and moderation, craved for ambassadors with independent minds and freedom of action, beyond their sovereigns' instructions.
49. Satow, *A Guide*, vol. 1, 174; Callières, *The Art of Diplomacy*, 111.
50. On the ideal diplomat see, Mattingly, *Renaissance Diplomacy*, 37–38, 201–212; Keens-Soper, "Wicquefort,", *Diplomacy and Statecraft* 8, 23; Anderson, *Modern Diplomacy*, 26–27, 45–46; Frey and Frey, *Diplomatic Immunity*, 128–130; Berridge, *Diplomatic Classics*, 63–4, 69–71, 90–96, 124–132; T. A. Baily, *The Art of Diplomacy* (New York: Meredith, 1968), 35–51, 63–78; Robert B. Mowat, *Diplomacy and Peace* (London: Williams and Norgate, 1935), 49–63; Wellesley, *Diplomacy in Fetters*, 204–216; Eban, *The New Diplomacy*, 376–381; William B. Macomber, *The Angels' Game: A Handbook of Modern Diplomacy* (London: Longman, 1975), 26–38; David Kelly, *The Ruling Few* (London: Hollis and Carter, 1952), 119; William Strang, *The Diplomatic Career* (London: Andre Deutsch, 1962), 9–33.
51. Callières, *The Art of Diplomacy*, 75–85, 151–154, 166–179. It is fair to note that Tocqueville, when arrived to France's Foreign Ministry in the mid-nineteenth century, did not have a high opinion of its diplomatic staff.
52. Ibid., 84, also 81–82.
53. Nicolson, *Diplomacy*, 51; also, Callières, *The Art of Diplomacy*, 168–169, 174.
54. Satow, *A Guide*, vol. 1, 157, 198–202; Berridge, Keens-Soper, and Otte, *Diplomatic Theory*, 132–133.
55. Harold Nicolson, *Diaries and Letters, 1930–1964*, Stanley, Osten (ed.) (New York: Atheneum, 1980), 301; also, Nicolson, *Diplomacy*, pp. 104–126, 144; Berridge, Keens-Soper, and Otte, *Diplomatic Theory*, pp. 165–167.

Chapter 3. Conventions and Rituals

1. Quoted in Keens-Soper, "Wicquefort," *Diplomacy and Statecraft* 8, 21.
2. See also, Norbert Elias, *The Civilizing Process* (Oxford: Blackwell, 1982), 319; Frey and Frey, *Diplomatic Immunity*, 108: "practice change, but only slowly."
3. John Searle, *The Construction of Social Reality* (London: Penguin, 1995), 1–7; also, Bull, *The Anarchical Society*, 304.

4. The establishment of immunity is best portrayed by Frey and Frey, *Diplomatic Immunity*, 4: "immunity was buttressed by religion, sanctioned by custom, and fortified by reciprocity"; Queller, "Medieval Diplomacy," in Jönsson and Langhorne, *Diplomacy*, vol. 2, 204; also, Satow, *A Guide*, vol. 1, 251–279; Michael Hardy, *Modern Diplomatic Law* (Manchester, UK: Manchester University Press, 1968), 41–49; Berridge, *Diplomacy, Theory and Practice*, 112–128.

5. Mattingly, *Renaissance Diplomacy*, 213–221, 256–281; the guarantee of safe passage was violated well into the beginning of the eighteenth century. Its most famous violation was Frederick II's capture of more than 100 archbishops, bishops, *nuncii*, and procurators, of prelates and ambassadors of the rebellious Lombard towns in 1241, Queller, "Medieval Diplomacy," in Jönsson and Langhorne, *Diplomacy*, vol. 2, 208–209; also, Frey and Frey, *Diplomatic Immunity*, 4–60, 75–86.

6. Frey and Frey, *Diplomatic Immunity*, 131; Anderson, *Modern Diplomacy*, 24–26, 53–56. The Duke of Milan, Francesco Sforza, executed a French agent in July 1533, and in 1511 Henry VIII had the papal envoy arrested for allegedly revealing secret information to the French ambassador.

7. Frey and Frey, *Diplomatic Immunity*, 291–327, 423–435. Edmond Burke referred to French diplomats as "emissaries of sedition." The Communist regimes of Russia and China limited the number of diplomats they would accept, and occasionally abused their immunity.

8. Satow, *A Guide*, vol. 1, 251–279; Barker, "The Theory and Practice," *Diplomacy and Statecraft* 6: 598–604; Richard Langhorne, "The Regulation of Diplomatic Practice: The Beginnings to the Vienna Convention on Diplomatic Relations, 1961," *Review of International Studies* 18 (1992), 3–17; The restriction of movement of diplomats collapsed by the end of the Cold War; Frey and Frey, *Diplomatic Immunity*, 336–374; Robert Harmon, *The Art and Practice of Diplomacy* (Metuchen: Scarecrow, 1971), 243–244.

9. Magalhães, *The Pure Concept of Diplomacy*, 103–126; Callières, *The Art of Diplomacy*, 110. The principal function of the diplomat is "to negotiate there the affairs of his own prince; and the other is to discover those of others"; The Vienna Convention refers to four functions: representing, protecting interests, reporting, and negotiating.

10. Dona Lee, "The Growing Influence of Business in United Kingdom Diplomacy," *International Studies Perspectives* 5 (2004), 50–54; Evan Potter, "Branding Canada: The Renaissance of Canada's Commercial Diplomacy," ibid., 55–60. Ambassadors were traditionally their countries' promotion officers, but certainly this does not change "the

identity of the diplomat"; Michael Lee, "British Cultural Diplomacy and the Cold War: 1946–1961," *Diplomacy and Statecraft* 9 (1998): 112–134; Berridge, *Diplomacy, Theory and Practice*, 187–203.

11. Callières, *The Art of Diplomacy*, 69, 110–117; Callières, writes, "It is hardly possible to conceal them [foreign affairs] from a prying minister who is upon the spot where they are forming"; Bull, *The Anarchical Society*, 170–172; Berridge, *Diplomacy, Theory and Practice*, 113; Kalevi Holsti, *International Politics: A Framework for Analysis* (Englewood Cliffs, NJ: Prentice Hall, 1992), 141–143; Robert H. Miller, *Inside an Embassy: The Political Role of Diplomats Abroad* (Washington, DC: Institute for the Study of Diplomacy, 1992), 2–13; Alan James, "Diplomacy and International Society," *International Relations* 6 (1980): 931–948.

12. Berridge, Keens-Soper, and Otte, *Diplomatic Theory*, 39–40, 77–78, 198; also, Barston, *Modern Diplomacy*, 84–89; Berridge, *Diplomacy, Theory and Practice*, 27–44; Jönsson and Hall, *Essence of Diplomacy*, 32–84; Satow, *A Guide*, vol. 1, 201–202, vol. 2, 344–345; Paul Meers, "The Changing Nature of Diplomatic Negotiation," in Melissen, *Innovation in Diplomatic Practice*, 79–92.

13. Satow, *A Guide*, vol. 1, 157; Jönsson and Hall, *Essence of Diplomacy*, 90–95; Berridge, *Diplomacy, Theory and Practice*, 89–102.

14. On these topics see, Christer Jönsson, and Martin Hall, "Communication: An Essential Aspect of Diplomacy," *International Studies Perspectives* 4 (2003): 195–210; Evan H. Potter, *Canada and the New Public Diplomacy* (Clingendael: The Netherlands Institute of International Relations, 2002); Jovan Kurbalija, "Diplomacy in the Age of Information Technology," in Melissen, *Innovation in Diplomatic Practice*, 171–189; Eytan Gilboa, "Diplomacy in the Media Age: Three Models of Uses and Effects," *Diplomacy and Statecraft* 12 (2001): 1–28; Costas M. Constantinou, Oliver Richmond, and Alison Watson, "International Relations and the Challenges of Global Communication," *Review of International Studies* 34 (2008): 1–19.

15. Abba Eban, *Diplomacy for the Next Century* (New Haven: Yale University Press, 1998), 82.

16. Christer Jönsson, "Diplomatic Signaling in the Television Age," in Jönsson and Langhorne, *Diplomacy*, vol. 3, 120–134; Eric Clark, *Corps Diplomatique* (London: A. Lane, 1973), 174–183; Jönsson and Hall, *Essence of Diplomacy*, 88–90; Brian Hocking, *Beyond "Newness" and "Decline": The Development of Catalytic Diplomacy* (Leicester, UK: University of Leicester, Centre for the Study of Diplomacy, 1995); Gary Rawnsley, *Radio Diplomacy and Propaganda: The BBC and VOA in International Politics, 1956–1964* (London: Macmillan, 1996).

17. Mowat, *Diplomacy and Peace*, 238–255; James Eayrs, *Diplomacy and Its Discontents* (Toronto: University of Toronto Press, 1971), 17–32; Anderson, *Modern Diplomacy*, 136–141.
18. Callières, *The Art of Diplomacy*, 157–158; Bull, *The Anarchical Society*, 179–180.
19. Antonia Fraser, *King Charles II* (London: Phoenix, 1979), 189; Charles W. Thayer , "Procedure and Protocol," in Elmer Plischke (ed.), *Modern Diplomacy: The Art and the Artisans* (Washington DC: American Enterprise Institute for Public Policy Research, 1979), 388–402.
20. Callières, *The Art of Diplomacy*, 106–108, 124–126; Sharp, *Diplomatic Theory*, 273; Costas M. Constantinou, *States of Political Discourse: Words, Regimes, Seditions* (London: Routledge, 2004), 86–98.
21. Jönsson and Hall, *Essence of Diplomacy*, 45–50; Berridge, *Diplomacy, Theory and Practice*, 101; Nicolson, *Diplomacy*, 178–201.
22. Shepard, "Information, Disinformation and Delay," in Jönsson and Langhorne, *Diplomacy*, vol. 2, 132–139; Bozeman, *Politics and Culture*, 308–309; Frey and Frey, *Diplomatic Immunity*, 208; Neumann, "Sublime Diplomacy," *Millennium* 34: 865–888.
23. Bernard Braudel, *A History of Civilization* (New York: Penguin, 1993), 42; Mukerjee, *Diplomacy*, 13; Mattingly, *Renaissance Diplomacy*, 35–37; Eban, *The New Diplomacy*, 337.
24. Kurt H. Wolff, (ed.), *Georg Simmel, 1858–1918* (Columbus: Ohio State University Press, 1955), 23; Z. D. Gurevitch, "Distance and Conversation," *Symbolic Interactions* 12 (1989): 251–263.
25. Norbert Elias, *The Court Society* (Oxford: Blackwell, 1983), 66–77, 78–116, 224–246; Elias, *The Civilizing Process*, 229–247.
26. Raymond Cohen, *The Theatre of Power* (London: Longman, 1987), 142—147; Clark, *Corps Diplomatique*, 109–115; John Wood, and Jean Serres, *Diplomatic Ceremonial and Protocol: Principles, Procedures and Practices* (New York: Columbia University Press, 1970), 3.
27. See also, Edward Muir, *Ritual in Early Modern Europe* (Cambridge: Cambridge University Press, 1997), 229–262; Satow, *A Guide*, vol. 1, 203–227; Wood and Serres, *Diplomatic Ceremonial*, 19–20, 81–83, 116–119, 122–125, 150–153; Cohen, *Theatre of Power*, 142–152; Ralph G. Feltham, – *Diplomatic Handbook* (London: Longman, 1970), 3–9, 19–23, 31–5, 44–7, 148–159.
28. Dorothy V. Jones, *Splendid Encounters: The Thought and Conduct of Diplomacy* (Chicago: The University of Chicago Library, 1984), 17–28, 46–48; Der Darian, *On Diplomacy*, 92, 117; Anderson, *Modern Diplomacy*, 15–6, 59–60; Hamilton and Langhorne, *The Practice of Diplomacy*, 47–49; Mattingly, *Renaissance Diplomacy*, 229–242; Queller, *Venetian Legislation*, 49.

29. Norman Rose, *Harold Nicolson: A Curious and Colorful Life* (London: Jonathan Cape, 2005), 145; Callières, *The Art of Diplomacy*, 116.

30. Muir, *Ritual*, 1–9; Elias, *Court Society*, 274; Frey and Frey, *Diplomatic Immunity*, 13, 39, 42, 47, 77; Lafont "International Relations in the Ancient Near East," *Diplomacy and Statecraft* 12: 51, 55; Cohen, "The Great Tradition," ibid., 23–38; Jönsson and Hall, *Essence of Diplomacy*, 42–44, 48–49.

Chapter 4. The Diplomatic Forum

1. Also, Erwing Goffman, *Behavior in Public Places* (New York: The Free Press, 1963); Frey and Frey, *Diplomatic Immunity*, 88.

2. Lafont, "International Relations in the Ancient Near East," *Diplomacy and Statecraft* 12: 47–49; Palmerston once quipped that "Dining is the soul of diplomacy."

3. Berridge, *Diplomatic Classics*, 28–29; Queller, "Medieval Diplomacy," 213; David Dunn (ed.), *Diplomacy at the Highest Level* (Basingstoke, UK: Macmillan, 1996), 3–22. The meeting between Napoleon and Alexander I of Russia in 1807 took place on a raft in the middle of the river Niemen.

4. Elias, *Court Society*, 52; Frey and Frey, *Diplomatic Immunity*, 196, 219–223, 225–250, 301–302.

5. Mowat, *Diplomacy and Peace*, 218–225.

6. Wolff, *Georg Simmel*, 23–27; Iver B. Neumann, "Self and Other in International Relations," *European Journal of International Relations* 2 (1996): 139–174.

7. See also, Z. D. Gurevitch, "The Power of Not Understanding: The Meeting of Conflicting Identities," *Journal of Applied Behavioral Science* 25 (1989): 161–173; Paul Hare, and Herbert Blumberg (eds.), *Dramaturgical Analysis of Social Interaction* (New York: Praeger, 1987), 4, 94; Erving Goffman, *Interaction Ritual* (Chicago: Aldine, 1967), 113–136.

8. Kurt Wolff (ed.), *The Sociology of Georg Simmel* (New York: The Free Press, 1950), 26–9, 40–55, 90–94, 105–114, 118–128.

9. Erik Goldstein, "The Origins of the Summit Diplomacy," in Dunn, *Diplomacy at the Highest Level*, 23–37.

10. Berridge, *Diplomatic Classics*, 25; Nicolson, *Peacemaking*, 207–208.

11. Jacek Bylica, "My Years with Gorbachev and Shevardnadze: A Memoir of a Soviet Interpreter by Pavel Palazchenko," *The Fletcher Forum of World Affairs* 22 (1998): 149–155.

12. On summitry see, Eban, *The New Diplomacy*, 358–364; Eban, *Diplomacy*

for the Next Century, 89–103; Elmer Plischke, *United States Department of State* (Westport: Greenwood Press, 1999), 278–279; F. Eilts, "Diplomacy—Contemporary Practice," in Plischke, *Modern Diplomacy*, 3–18; Elmer Plischke "Summit Diplomacy—Diplomat in Chief," ibid., 180–185; Berridge, Keens-Soper and Otte, *Diplomatic Theory*, 136, 161, 168, 201–202; Dunn, *Diplomacy at the Highest Level*, 3–22, 247–268.

13. Robert Dallek, *John F. Kennedy. An Unfinished Life 1917–1963* (London: Penguin, 2004), 401–414; Charles E. Bohlen, *Witness to History, 1929–1969* (New York: Norton, 1973), 399–403.

14. Johan Kaufmann, *Conference Diplomacy* (London: Macmillan, 1996); John McDonald, *How to Be a Delegate: International Conference Diplomacy* (Washington DC: The Institute for Multi-Track Diplomacy, 1994); Barston, *Modern Diplomacy*, 88–89, 169; Satow, *A Guide*, vol. 2, 1–91, 100–197; Hamilton and Langhorne, *The Practice of Diplomacy*, 158–169; Berridge, *Diplomacy, Theory and Practice*, 145–164.

15. Wolff, *The Sociology of Georg Simmel*, 127, 135–138; Nicolson, *Diplomacy*, 198, 201.

16. Berridge, *Diplomatic Classics*, 85; Callières, *The Art of Diplomacy*, 96–100; Satow, *A Guide*, vol. 1, 145; Nicolson, *Diplomacy*, 104–126; Mark A. Boyer, "Moving Targets: Understanding Diplomacy and Negotiation in a Globalizing System," *International Studies Review* 3 (2001), 91–99.

17. Bertolt Brecht , *Brecht on Theatre*, John Willet (ed.) (New York: Hill and Wang, 1964), 19–95; Keens-Soper, "Wicquefort," *Diplomacy and Statecraft* 8: 22; Berridge, *Diplomatic Classics*, 129; also, Constantinou, *Diplomacy*, 95–103; Callières, *The Art of Diplomacy*, 76–77.

18. Jönnson and Hall, *Essence of Diplomacy*, 84–88, 119–131; Cohen, *The Theatre of Power*, 1–40, 108–109.

19. Willem Mastenbreak, "Negotiation as Emotion Management," *Theory, Culture and Society* 16 (1999): 49–73; David Clinton, "Emotion and Calculation: Callières and Bismarck," paper presented at the International Studies Association Convention, Montreal, March 2004; Neta C. Crawford, "The Passion of World Politics," *International Security* 24 (2000): 116–156.

20. G. R. Berridge, "Diplomacy After Death: The Rise of the Working Funeral," *Diplomacy and Statecraft* 2 (1993): 217–234; Erik Goldstein, "The Politics of the State Visit," *Diplomacy and Statecraft* 12 (1997): 1–28. In the case of President Wilson's visit to England in December 1918, the results were counterproductive. Both King George V and Lloyd George were disenchanted by the president's personality.

21. Douglas Busk, *The Craft of Diplomacy* (London: Paul Mall, 1967), 16–17; Piers Dixon, *Double Diploma* (London: Hutchinson, 1968), 152.

22. Miller, *Inside an Embassy*, 118–120. In a dispatch of July 10, 1973, Ambassador Robert Miller recorded his meeting with General Idi Amin, ruler of Uganda. After a forty-minute wait, he was ushered in for a meeting that lasted twenty minutes. It was mainly a one-way lecture, while the scene was filmed for TV; Kissinger, *The White House Years*, 708–713. The ping-pong diplomacy, initiated by Chou En-Lai, symbolized China's commitment to improve relations with the United States.

23. Karin Aggestam, *Reframing and Resolving Conflict. Israel-Palestine Negotiations 1988–1998* (Lund, Sweden: Lund University Press, 1999), 131–146; Berridge, *Diplomatic Classics*, 1–15.

24. On negotiations see, Rose, *Nicolson*, 88–89. Simon Bolivar's advice for negotiations-Calm, Delay, Compliments, Vague words and be very laconic; Holsti, *International Politics*,145–155; William Zartman, *Negotiations as a Mechanism for Resolution in the Arab-Israeli Conflict* (Jerusalem: The Leonard Davis Institute for International Relations, 1999). Zartman highlights the importance of ripeness; Callières, *The Art of Diplomacy*, 145–149; Berridge, *Diplomacy, Theory and Practice*, 27–44, 46–54, 56–64, 187–203; Barston, *Modern Diplomacy*, 84–89; Berridge, *Diplomatic Classics*, 2–4, 84–85, 117–118, 164–165.

25. Raymond Cohen, *Negotiations Across Cultures* (Washington, DC: United States Institute of Peace Press, 1991), 7–32.

26. Berridge, *Diplomatic Classics*, 91, 164; Berridge, Keens-Soper, and Otte, *Diplomatic Theory*, 198–199; Callières, *The Art of Diplomacy*, 164; Eban, *The New Diplomacy*, 346, 393.

27. Queller, *Venetian Legislation*, 44, 57; Mattingly, *Renaissance Diplomacy*, 231–238; Nevile Henderson, *Water Under the Bridges* (London: Hodder and Stoughton, 1945), 29–31.

28. Quoted in Wight, *International Theory*, 199–205; On secrecy see, Wolff, *The Sociology of Georg Simmel*, 295–298; Strang, *The Diplomatic Career*, 76–81; Watson, *Diplomacy*, 64, 138–139; Berridge, Keens-Soper, and Otte, *Diplomatic Theory*, 41, 78, 134, 140, 164, 198; Wellesley, *Diplomacy in Fetters*, 16; Berridge, *Diplomacy, Theory and Practice*, 67–68; Jones, *Splendid Encounters*, 47–51. The first printed work on cryptology was published in 1513; L. N. Rangarajan, "Diplomacy, States and Secrecy in Communication," *Diplomacy and Statecraft* 9 (1998): 18–49.

Chapter 5. Credentials of Words

1. Mattingly, *Renaissance Diplomacy*, 38; Bull, *The Anarchical Society*, 179–180; Watson, *Diplomacy*, 215; Gurevitch, "The Power of Not Understanding," *Journal of Applied Behavioral Science* 25, 161–162.

2. Nicolson, *Diplomacy*, 96–101; Nicolson, *Peacemaking*, 209; Wellesley, *Diplomacy in Fetters*, 211.

3. Mattingly, *Renaissance Diplomacy*, 227; Bailey, *The Art of Diplomacy*, 48; Black, *A History of Diplomacy*, 70; Hamilton and Langhorne, *The Practice of Diplomacy*, 48.

4. Ross, *Leibniz*, 24; Richard Tuck, *The Rights of War and Peace* (Oxford: Oxford University Press, 1999), 167; Mattingly, *Renaissance Diplomacy*, 273; David Armitage, "John Locke's International Thought," in Ian Hall and Lisa Hill (eds.), *British International Thinkers from Hobbes to Namier* (New York: Palgrave, Macmillan, 2009), 33–49.

5. Dixon, *Double Diploma*, 18; *International Herald Tribune*, March 19–20, 2005; one may add the names of Octavio Paz, Czeslaw Milosz, and the Dutch F. Springer.

6. Rose, *Nicolson*, 136, 251–252; Mowat, *Diplomacy and Peace*, 271.

7. Pablo Neruda, *Memoirs* (Harmondsworth, UK: Penguin, 1982), 65–66.

8. Elizabeth Cameron, "Alexis Saint-Léger," in Gordon Craig, and Felix Gilbert (eds.), *The Diplomats 1919–1939* (New York: Atheneum, 1968), 376–405.

9. Satow, *A Guide*, vol. 1, 79; Salvador De Madaraiga, *Englishmen, Frenchmen, Spaniards* (Oxford: Oxford University Press, 1928).

10. On diplomatic correspondence see, Nicolson, *Diplomacy*, 192–194; Mowat, *Diplomacy and Peace*, 50; Satow, *A Guide*, vol. 2, 79–108, 250–208, 270–295; Wood and Serres, *Diplomatic Ceremonial*, 185–209; Barston, *Modern Diplomacy*, 43–81; Ivone Kirkpatrick, *The Inner Circle* (London: Macmillan, 1959), 210–213; Written reports became customary already in Byzantine diplomacy. Instructions for ambassadors in Royal France were known for their literary elegance.

11. See also, Iver B. Neumann, "A Speech that the Entire Ministry May Stand For: Or, Why Diplomats Never Produce Anything New," *International Political Sociology*1 (2007): 183–200; George F. Kennen, *Memoirs, 1925–1950* (Boston: Little Brown, 1967), 20.

12. Eban, *The New Diplomacy*, 391–394; Reus-Smit, *The Moral Purpose*, 80.

13. See Jovan Kurbalija, and Hanna Slavik (eds.), *Language and Diplomacy* (Malta: Mediterranean Academy of Diplomatic Studies, 2001); Chas Freeman, "Lingua Diplomatica," *Foreign Policy* (November-December, 2002), 84–88; Iver B. Neumann, "Returning Practice to the Linguistic Turn: The Case of Diplomacy," *Millennium* 31 (2002): 627–651.

14. Raymond Cohen, "Meaning, Interpretation and International Negotiation," *Global Society* 14 (2000): 317–335; Aharon Kleiman, *Constructive Ambiguity in Middle-East Peace-Making* (Tel Aviv: The Tami Steinmetz Center for Peace Research, 1999); Ilai Alon, *Negotiations*

in Arabic-Speaking Islam (Jerusalem: The Leonard Davis Institute for International Relations, Hebrew University, 2000). Raymond Cohen, "Language and Conflict Resolution: The Limits of English," *International Studies Review* 3 (2001): 25–51; Carne Ross, *Independent Diplomat. Dispatches from an Unaccountable Elite* (Ithaca: Cornell University Press, 2007), 104, 157–162.

15. George Rendel, *The Sword and the Olive* (London: John Murray, 1957), 93–94; Mattingly, *Renaissance Diplomacy*, 225–226; Nicolson, *Diplomatic Method*, 56–57; Hamilton and Langhorne, *The Practice of Diplomacy*, 105–107, 157.

16. Berridge, *Diplomacy, Theory and Practice*, 64–67; Nicolson, *Diplomacy*, 219–243; Raymond Cohen, *International Negotiations: A Semantic Analysis* (Leicester, UK: University of Leicester, Centre for the Study of Diplomacy, 1999).

17. Brian Harris, "Ernest Satow's Early Career as Diplomatic Interpreter," *Diplomacy and Statecraft* 13 (2002): 116–134.

18. Callières, *The Art of Diplomacy*, 157; Nicolson, *Peacemaking*, 207–208; Nicolson, *The Congress of Vienna*, 177; Talleyrand accused Metternich of a "command of Words that are vague and void of meaning."

19. See, Satow, *A Guide*, vol. 1, 190, 232–233; Harmon, *The Art and Practice of Diplomacy*, 224–231; Callières, *The Art of Diplomacy*, 101, 153; Barston, *Modern Diplomacy*, 18–26.

20. On Precedence see, Wight, *Power Politics*, 38–39; Satow, *A Guide*, vol. 1, 22–29, 122–136, 237–248; Callières, *The Art of Diplomacy*, 124–129; Anderson, *Modern Diplomacy*, 62–63; Hamilton and Langhorne, *The Practice of Diplomacy*, 64–68; when Peter the Great assumed the title of an Emperor it aroused the objection of the Habsburgs as the Emperors of the Holy Roman Empire.

21. See Wood and Serres, *Diplomatic Ceremonial*, 81–85, 94–85; Nicolson, *The Congress of Vienna*, 217–220. The règlement of the Vienna Congress divided diplomatic representatives into four ranks: ambassadors and Papal legates, ministers plenipotentiary, minister resident, and chargés d'affairs. The Conference of Aix-la-Chapelle decided that signatures of treaties should be in alphabetical order.

22. Charles H. Carter, "The Ambassadors of Early Modern Europe: Patterns of Diplomatic Representation in the Early Seventeenth Century," in Jönsson and Langhorne (eds.), *Diplomacy*, vol. 2, 232–250; Berridge, *Diplomacy, Theory and Practice*, 117–118, 132–142; Harmon, *The Art and Practice of Diplomacy*, 223–292; Hardy, *Modern Diplomatic Law*, 19; The Vienna Convention divided the personnel of diplomatic missions into three categories: diplomatic agents, administrative and technical staff, and service staff.

23. See also Costas M. Constantinou, "Diplomatic Representations . . . Or Who Framed the Ambassadors?" *Millennium* 23 (1994): 1–23; Paul Sharp, "For Diplomacy: Representation and the Study of International Relations," *International Studies Review* 1 (1999), 33–57.
24. Callières, *The Art of Diplomacy*, 174–177; Wellesley, *Diplomacy in Fetters*, 208, 212.
25. Constantinou, "Diplomatic Representations," Millennium, 1–23; see also Satow, *A Guide*, vol. 1, 221.

Chapter 6. Diplomats and Their Milieu

1. See Thomas Munck, *Seventeenth Century Europe, 1598–1700* (London: Macmillan, 1990), 137–164; Anderson, *Modern Diplomacy*, 89–90; Jeremy Black, *Eighteenth Century Europe* (London: Macmillan, 1999), 125–142; Black, *A History of Diplomacy*, 72–73.
2. Lawrence Stone, *The Crisis of the Aristocracy, 1558–1641* (Oxford: Oxford University Press, 1965), 107–108, 459–462.
3. See Noel Annan, *Our Age* (London: Weidenfeld and Nicolson, 1990).
4. Kelly, *The Ruling Few*, 47–50, 76–77; see also, Dixon, *Double Diploma*, 1–26; Lord Hardinge of Penshurst, *Old Diplomacy* (London: John Murray, 1947); his father was an undersecretary at the War Office; Martin Gilbert, *Sir Horace Rumbold* (London: Heinemann, 1973), 2–9. Rumbold's ancestors had been in the public service for more than three centuries; Norman Rose, *Vansittart: A Study of a Diplomat* (London: Heinemann, 1978), 4–25.
5. Keens-Soper, "Wicquefort," *Diplomacy and Statecraft* 8: 23; Callières, *The Art of Diplomacy*, 166; Nicolson, *Diplomatic Method*, 34; Nicolson, *Diplomacy*, 51.
6. John Clarke, *British Diplomacy and Foreign Policy, 1782–1865* (London: Unwin Hyman, 1989), 45–53; Hamilton and Langhorne, *The Practice of Diplomacy*, 98–105; Anderson, *Modern Diplomacy*, 32–40; Satow, *A Guide*, vol. 1, 8–16.
7. Eayers, *Diplomacy*, 114–115; Neumann, "A Speech that the Entire Ministry May Stand For," *International Political Sociology* 1: 183–200.
8. Geoffrey A. Pigman, *Contemporary Diplomacy* (Cambridge: Polity, 2010), 33–39; Harry Kopp and Charles Gillespie, *Career Diplomacy, Life and Work in the United States Foreign Service* (Washington, DC: Georgetown University Press, 2008), 3–10; Plischke, *U.S. Department of State*, 13–19, 211. The Roger Act of 1924 established the charter for a career service. Not until 1893 did Congress authorize the appointment of American diplomats at the rank of ambassador; see also *Háaretz*, June 27, 2006; *International Herald Tribune*, December

18, 2003. In 2003, the Quai d'Orsay employed a permanent staff of 9,200; the German Foreign Ministry employed 11,650; and the Israeli Foreign Ministry about 1,200.

9. Callières, *The Art of Diplomacy*, 189–215. The academy collapsed in 1721.

10. Paul G. Lauren, *Diplomats and Bureaucrats* (Palo Alto: Stanford University Press, 1976); Nicolson, *Diplomacy*, 202–218.

11. Monteagle Stearns, *Talking to Strangers* (Princeton: Princeton University Press, 1996), 35; Robert Schulzinger, *The Making of the Diplomatic Mind* (Middletown, CN: Wesleyan University Press, 1975), 81–111, 152–155.

12. John Hemery, "Educating Diplomats," *International Studies Perspectives* 3 (2002): 140–145; Kopp and Gillespie, *Career Diplomacy*, 135–149; Busk, *The Craft of Diplomacy*, 183–227; Anderson, *Modern Diplomacy*, 123–134.

13. See, Grey, *Twenty-Five Years*, 43; Rose, *Vansittart*, 4–25; B. J. C. McKercher, "The Last Old Diplomat: Sir Robert Vansittart and the Verities of British Foreign Policy, 1903–1930," *Diplomacy and Statecraft* 6 (1995): 4–7; Rendel, *The Sword and the Olive*, 1–3; Henderson, *Water Under the Bridges*, 20–23; Kirkpatrick, *The Inner Circle*, 1–29; Valentine Lawford, *Bound for Diplomacy* (London: John Murray, 1963), 224–240; Harris, "Ernest Satow's Early Career," *Diplomacy and Statecraft* 13: 116–134; Gilbert, *Rumbold*, 2–9.

14. Adam Feinstein, *Pablo Neruda* (London: Bloomsbury, 2004), 57–67.

15. Joseph C. Grew, *Turbulent Era*, E. Johnson (ed.) (London: Hammond, 1953), vol. 1, 6–14.

16. Kennan, *Memoirs*, vol. 1, 9–23.

17. Bohlen, *Witness to History*, 3–13; Kirkpatrick, *The Inner Circle*, 260; see also Peter Bridges, "On the Isthmus: A Young American at the Panama Embassy, 1959–1961," *Diplomacy and Statecraft* 9 (1998): 184–197.

18. Henderson, *Water Under Bridges*, 84–85.

19. Nicolson, *Diaries and Letters*, 36–37, 80; Rose, *Nicolson*, 136–137, 152–165.

20. Lorna Lloyd, "Diplomats: A Breed Apart or Anyone Goes? The Question of Political Appointees as Head of Missions," paper presented at the Annual Convention of the International Studies Association, San Diego, March 2006; Kopp and Gillespie, *Career Diplomacy*, 51–52; *New York Times*, February 8, 2007.

21. Schulzinger, *The Diplomatic Mind*, 108–109; Busk, *The Craft of Diplomacy*, 203–206; *New York Times*, August 12, 2009.

22. Berridge, *Diplomatic Classics*, 96–97; Kopp and Gillespie, *Career Diplomacy*, 20–23; Plischke, *U.S. Department of State*, 512–519.

23. *History Notes: Women in Diplomacy. The FCO, 1782–1994* (London: History Branch, LRD no. 6, 1994); Iver B. Neumann, "The Body of the Diplomat," *European Journal of International Relations* 14 (2008), 671–695; Jean-Robert Leguey-Feilleux, *The Dynamics of Diplomacy* (Boulder: Lynne Reinner, 2009), 147–152.

24. Philip Nash, "America's First Female Chief of Mission: Ruth Bryan Owen, Minister to Denmark, 1933–36: *Diplomacy and Statecraft* 16 (2005): 52–72; Philip Nash, "A Woman's Touch in Foreign Affairs? The Career of Ambassador Frances E. Willis," *Diplomacy and Statecraft* 13 (2002): 1–20.

25. Kennan, *Memoirs*, vol. 2, 323; Kelley, *The Ruling Few*, 2; Kopp and Gillespie, *Career Diplomacy*, 7; also, George F. Kennan, "Diplomacy Without Diplomats," *Foreign Affairs* 76 (1997), 199–212.

26. Queller, *Venetian Legislation*, 23–25; Frey and Frey, *Diplomatic Immunity*, 207–249; Linda Frey and Marsha Frey, "International Officials and the Standard of Diplomatic Privilege," *Diplomacy and Statecraft* 9 (1998): 1–17.

27. Dixon, *Double Diploma*, 85, 143. Dixon's entire diary is scattered with remarks on the quality of drink and food; also, John E. Harr, *The Professional Diplomat* (Princeton: Princeton University Press, 1969), 204–207, 254–257; Rose, *Nicolson*, 136. Edmund Wilson blamed Nicolson's aristocratic origins and diplomatic life for his failure as a writer: "well-brushed and well-bred he has no conception of any other kind of life"; Macomber, *The Angels' Game*, 35. Quotes the American ambassador to London, Charles Dawes, "Diplomacy is easy on the head but hell on the feet." It is worth also to quote Rumbold's description of the Foreign Office premises: "dingy and shabby to a degree, made up of dark offices and labyrinthine passages—four houses at least tumbled into one, with floors at uneven levels and wearing corkscrew stairs that men cursed as they climbed—a thorough picture of disorder, penury and meanness," Clarke, *British Diplomacy*, 47.

28. Frey and Frey, *Diplomatic Immunity*, 480–495; *New York Times*, February 24, 2007, French and American diplomats' resistance over London traffic changes.

29. Also, Zara S. Steiner, *The Foreign Office and Foreign Policy 1898–1914* (Cambridge: Cambridge University Press, 1969), 172–183; Kennan, *Memoirs*, vol. 1, 91–92; Kennan on Joseph Kennedy's demand to assist his son John in his study tour of Europe; Harr, *The Professional Diplomat*, 292–294.

30. Katie Hickman, *Daughters of Britannia: The Lives and Times of Diplomatic Wives* (London: Flamingo, 2000), 1–47; Clark, *Corps Diplomatique*, 92–97; Berridge, *Diplomatic Classics*, 15, 96–97; Wood and

Serres, *Diplomatic Ceremonial*, 147–149; Wellesley, *Diplomacy in Fetters*, 18–19.

31. Cynthia Enloe, *Bananas, Beaches and Bases* (Albany: State University of New York Press, 1990), 93–123. In 1972, the State Department recognized spouses as "private persons to be treated as unpaid employees"; Annabel Black, "The Changing Culture of Diplomatic Spouses: Some Field Notes from Brussels," *Diplomacy and Statecraft* 6 (1995): 196–222; *New York Times*, May 2, 2009, "Diplomats' Same-Sex Partners to Get Benefits."

32. See also, Dixon, *Double Diploma*, 95. The books of the Dutch writer and former diplomat Carel Jan Schneider testify to the melancholy and uprooting of diplomatic life.

33. Callières, *The Art of Diplomacy*, 98; Dixon, *Double Diploma*, 39; Black, *A History of Diplomacy*, 96–97; Anderson, *Modern Diplomacy*, 26–28, 52–53.

34. Kirkpatrick, *The Inner Circle*, 269, "To leave a service in which one has spent one's life is rather like dying."

35. T. G. Otte, "'Not Proficient in Table-Thumbing'": Sir Ernest Satow in Peking, 1900–1906," *Diplomacy and Statecraft*, 13 (2002): 229–243; Gilbert, *Rumbold*, 387–388.

36. Rendel, *The Sword and the Olive*, 269.

37. Kennan, *Memoirs*, vol. 1, 134–137; Nicolson, *Diplomatic Method*, 56; Lady Algernon Gordon Lenox (ed.), *The Dairy of Lord Bertie*, vol. 1 (London: Hodder and Stoughton, 1924), 16; Frey and Frey, *Diplomatic Immunity*, 133–135; Walter Orebaugh (with Carol Jose), *The Consul* (Cape Canaveral: Blue Note, 1994), the war adventures of the American Consul in Nice during the Second World War.

38. Kopp and Gillespie, *Career Diplomacy*, 23–31, 53; Frey and Frey, *Diplomatic Immunity*, 479–526; see also, Joseph Sullivan (ed.), *Embassies Under Siege* (Washington, DC: Brassey's, 1995), 35–53; Craig J. Barker, *The Abuse of Diplomatic Privileges and Immunities* (Dartmouth: Aldershot, 1996); Leguey-Feilleux, *The Dynamics of Diplomacy*, 161–167; *New York Times*, September 9, 2012. Protesters attacked the American embassies in Sana, Cairo, and Lybia, where assailants killed four Americans including the Ambassador Christopher J. Stevens.

39. On the diplomatic corps see, Paul Sharp, and Geoffrey Wiseman (eds.), *The Diplomatic Corps as an Institution of International Society* (Houndmills, UK: Palgrave, Macmillan, 2007).

40. See also, Mattingly, *Renaissance Diplomacy*, 100; Satow, *A guide*, vol. 1, 352–375; Wood and Serres, *Diplomatic Ceremonial*, 29–31, 35–43, 110–118; Berridge, *Diplomatic Classics*, 14–15, 170–172.

41. Quoted in Hickman, *Daughters of Britannia*, 272.

42. See also, Hamilton and Langhorne, *The Practice of Diplomacy*, 105; Busk, *The Craft of Diplomacy*, 2–3.

43. David Armstrong, *Revolutionary Diplomacy* (Leicester, UK: Centre for the Study of Diplomacy, 1996), 14; Clark, *Corps Diplomatique*, 18; Callières, *The Art of Diplomacy*, 116, 187; Watson, *Diplomacy*, 128–131; Nicholas Henderson, "The Washington Embassy: Navigating the Waters of the Potomac," *Diplomacy and Statecraft* 1 (1990): 40–48, advises diplomats not to invest too much in meetings with State Department's officials.

44. See also, G. R. Berridge and N. Gallo, "The Role of the Diplomatic Corps: The US-North Korea Talks in Beijing, 1988–94," in Melissen, *Innovation in Diplomatic Practice*, 214–226.

45. Nicolson, *Diplomacy*, 127–153; De Madaraiga, *Englishmen, Frenchmen, Spaniards*, 3. His concise description of their corresponding national character–the English, fair play; the French, *le droit*, the Spanish, *el honor*.

46. See also, Sharp, *Diplomatic Theory*, 107; Watson, *Diplomacy*, 131; Berridge, *Diplomatic Classics*, 161, 170; Abba Eban, *An Autobiography* (New York: Random House, 1977), 590–610.

Chapter 7. The Courtiers of Civilization

1. See, de Magalhães, *The Pure Concept of Diplomacy*, 31–34; Watson, *Diplomacy*, 86; Donald E. Queller, *The Office of Ambassador in the Middle Ages* (Princeton: Princeton University Press, 1967); Mattingly, *Renaissance Diplomacy*, 201; Der Derian, *On Diplomacy*, 80–95.

2. Quoted in Macomber, *The Angels' Game*, 19.

3. See Satow, *A Guide*, vol. 1, 181–183; Callières, *The Art of Diplomacy*, 128; Frey and Frey, *Diplomatic Immunity*, 14–15, 294–295; Mattingly, *Renaissance Diplomacy*, 249.

4. Felix Gilbert, "The 'New Diplomacy' of the Eighteenth Century," *World Politics* 4 (1951): 1–38; Sharp, *Diplomatic Theory*, 19–38; Frey and Frey, *Diplomatic Immunity*, 321–322. Thomas Paine argued that diplomacy based on the reciprocity of suspicion forbids a true human intercourse; Armstrong, *Revolutionary Diplomacy* (Leicester Centre for the Study of Diplomacy), 3; diplomats as attached to the status quo, stability and aristocratic origins, were detested by revolutionaries.

5. Eban, *Diplomacy for the Next Century*, 40; Eban, *Autobiography*, 591; George F. Kennan, *Memoirs, 1950–1963* (Boston: Little and Brown, 1972), 319–21; also, Anderson, *Modern Diplomacy*, 13–14, 45–46,

230–232; Nicolson, *Peacemaking*, 209, "diplomacy if it is ever to be effective, should be a disagreeable business."

6. British writers, particularly those of some service in undercover missions, adopted an attitude of distrust and nihilist disregard toward diplomats; it is of interest to note that notable writers on diplomacy, including Machiavelli, Grotius, Wicquefort, Callières, and Nicolson, were all frustrated with their diplomatic careers. Notorious, in this regard, was Grotius, described by King James I as "some pedant, full of words and of no great judgement"; see, Renée Jeffrey, *Hugo Grotius in International Relations* (Harmondsworth, UK: Palgrave, Macmillan, 2006), 8–9, 14; Kopp and Gillespie, *Career Diplomacy*, 11.

7. Leo Tolstoy, *Anna Karenina* (Mineola, NY: Dover, 2004), 116–122, 611–614.

8. Virginia Woolf, *Orlando* (Harmondsworth, UK: Penguin, 1993), 84–94; Hickman, *Daughters of Britannia*, 12; see also, Constantinou, *States of Political Discourse*, 86–98.

9. Gilbert, *Rumbold*, 178–181.

10. See also, Der Derian, *On Diplomacy*, 4; Wellesley, *Diplomacy in Fetters*, 210; Mattingly, *Renaissance Diplomacy*, 256; Sharp, *Diplomatic Theory*, 53–71, 103; Von Bismarck, *Reflections*, vol. 2, 175–182; Count Harry von Arnim, the ambassador to Paris, regarded his post as a stepping-stone in his attempt to replace Bismarck. In 1873, he refused to obey Bismarck's official instructions. He was tried and imprisoned.

11. A. J. P. Taylor, *The Struggle for Mastery in Europe* (London: Oxford University Press, 1971), XXXIII; Taylor, *Europe*, 354.

12. Anthony Eden, *Full Circle: The Memoirs of Lord Avon* (London: Cassell, 1960), 357; see also, Alfred Vagts, *Defense and Diplomacy* (New York: King's Crown Press, 1956), 1–9.

13. Nicolson, *Diplomacy*, 117.

14. Sebastian De Grazia, *Machiavelli in Hell* (New York: Vintage Books, 1994), 210.

15. Berridge, *Diplomatic Classics*, 69–71, 124–132; Mattingly, *Renaissance Diplomacy*, 209.

16. Callières, *The Art of Diplomacy*, 77, 132, 135, 139, 147, 150–154.

17. Knecht, *Richelieu*, 13–16, 212–215. For centuries the "red tyrant" was vilified by French writers, including Alexandre Dumas in *The Three Musketeers*; see also, Munck, *Seventeenth Century Europe*, 43.

18. Nicolson, *Diplomatic Method*, 54–55; Munck, *Seventeenth Century Europe*, 372; Kissinger, *A World Restored*, 147–149, 167–168.

19. Wight, *International Theory*, 147, Palmerston quipped that, "When I wish to be misinformed about a country I ask the man who has lived

there thirty years"; Black, *A History of Diplomacy*, 182; Lawford, *Bound for Diplomacy*, 271–272; Roderick R. McLean, *Royalty and Diplomacy in Europe, 1890–1914* (Cambridge, UK: Cambridge University Press, 2001), 128–129, 141–148, 177–183; Mowat, *Diplomacy and Peace*, 79–87.

20. Rose, *Vansittart*, 88–102; Berridge, Keens-Soper, and Otte, *Diplomatic Theory*, 162; Gordon A. Craig, and Alexander George, *Force and State-craft* (Oxford: Oxford University Press, 1982), 65–67; McKercher, "The Last Old Diplomat," *Diplomacy and Statecraft* 6: 10–29; Leonard Mosley, *Curzon* (London: Longmans and Greene, 1961), 128–129, 201–220.

21. Edward Corp, "Sir Eyre Crowe and George Clemenceau at the Paris Peace Conference, 1919–20," *Diplomacy and Statecraft* 8 (1997): 10–19; ultimately, Crowe served as a permanent undersecretary in the years 1920–1925.

22. Henderson, *Water Under the Bridges*, 210–213; Goldstein, "The Origins of Summit Diplomacy," in Dunn, *Diplomacy at the Highest Level*, 23–37; Kirkpatrick, *The Inner Circle*, 112–127.

23. Rose, *Vansittart*, 199–214.

24. Andrew Roberts, *The Holy Fox: Biography of Lord Halifax* (London: Widenfeld and Nicolson, 1991), 273–280; Eayers, *Diplomacy*, 124.

25. Peter Bridges, "Eugene Schuyler, the Only Diplomatist," *Diplomacy and Statecraft* 16 (2005): 13–22; David H. Donald *Lincoln* (London: Jonathan Cape, 1995), 412.

26. Grew, *Turbulent Era*, vol. 1, 13.

27. Stearns, *Talking to Strangers*, 74–75; Kopp and Gillespie, *Career Diplomacy*, 88–117.

28. Kissinger, *The White House Years*, vol. 1, 27–28; Kissinger went to China in 1971 without giving the slightest warning to either the State or the Defense Departments, or the Congress.

29. See also, Stearns, *Talking to Stranger*, 74–75; Peter Collier, and David Horowitz, *The Kennedys* (New York: Warner, 1984), 86–87; William Kaufmann, "The American Ambassadors: Bullitt and Kennedy," in Craig and Gilbert, *The Diplomats*, 649–681.

30. Jean E. Smith, *FDR* (New York: Random House, 2007), 486, 497–498, 582–587; Dean Acheson, *Present at the Creation: My Years at the State Department* (London: Norton, 1969), 9–11, 18; Wight, *International Theory*, 156–157.

31. Arthur Schlesinger, *A Thousand Days: John F. Kennedy at the White House* (Boston: Houghton Mifflin, 1965), 406, 434–436,; Dallek, *Kennedy*, 160, 314–315, 369–370, 456; Douglas Little, "Crackpot Realists and Other Heroes: The Rise and Fall of the Post-War American

Diplomatic Elite," *Diplomacy and Statecraft* 13 (2002): 99–112; Evan Thomas, *Robert Kennedy* (New York: Simon and Schuster, 2000), 122, 134, 139, 189; Ted Sorensen, *The Counselor* (New York: Harper Perennial, 2008),233–235.

32. Geoffrey McDermott, *The New Diplomacy* (London: The Plume Press, 1973), 28–30; Kopp and Gillespie, *Career Diplomacy*, 10–19, 88–111.

33. The list may include Crowe and Vansittart in Great Britain; Joseph Grew, Averell Harriman, Ralph Bunch, and Richard Holbrooke in the United States; Abba Eban of Israel; and the Russians Chicherin, Litvinov, Gromyko, and Dobrynin.

34. Kennan, *Memoirs*, vol. 1, 290–207; Kennan, *Memoirs*, vol. 2, 100; Kissinger, *Diplomacy*, 447–449, 454–456, 463–466.

35. Kennan, *Memoirs*, vol. 2, 168–189; Kennan, "Diplomacy Without Diplomats," *Foreign Affairs*, 76, 201; George F. Kennan, *At Century's Ending* (New York: Norton, 1996), 135–136.

36. Kennan, *Memoirs*, vol. 2, 200–215; Harr, *The Professional Diplomat*, 36.

37. Der Derian, *On Diplomacy*, 6, 8–29, 42.

38. Georg Simmel, "The Stranger," in *Georg Simmel on Individuality and Social Forms*, Donald Levine (ed.) (Chicago: University of Chicago Press, 1972), 143–149; Alfred Schuetz, "The Stranger: An Essay in Social Psychology," *American Journal of Sociology* 49 (1944): 499–507.

39. See also, Gurevitch, "Distance and Conversation," *Symbolic Interaction* 12: 256; Constantinou, *On the Way to Diplomacy*, 110–120.

40. See also, Von Bismarck, *Reflections*, vol. 2, 229.

41. Henderson, *Water Under the Bridges*, 23. Henderson wrote further, "I was a Scot who had lived in exile all my life, first at school in England and afterwards abroad in the service of my country."

42. Averell Harriman (and Elie Abel), *Special Envoy to Churchill and Stalin, 1941–1946* (New York: Random House, 1975), 545; Kennan, *Memoirs*, vol. 2, 61–62; see also, Strang, *The Diplomatic Career*, 18–19; Eban, *The New Diplomacy*, 367–368.

43. Callières, *The Art of Diplomacy*, 86–9, 139–143, 150; Nicolson, *Diplomacy*, 116–117; see also, Der Derian, *On Diplomacy*, 167, 209, 297; Neumann, "Self and Other," *European Journal of International Relations* 2: 139–174.

44. Callières, *The Art of Diplomacy*, 153.

45. Kennan, *Memoirs*, vol. 1, 20.

46. Nicolson, *Diaries*, 33.

47. See also, Kissinger, *A World Restored*, 10; Berridge, Keens-Soper, and Otte, *Diplomatic Theory*, 186; Der Derian, *On Diplomacy*, 85–100; Sharp, *Diplomatic Theory*, 191–192, 195–196, to think diplomatically is unique and separate from thinking politically.

48. See also, Searle, *The Construction of Social Reality*, 8; Rendel, *The Sword and the Olive*, 45–46.
49. Bull, *The Anarchical Society*, 172; Eban, *The New Diplomacy*, 356; Callières, *The Art of Diplomacy*, 132–133.
50. Nicolson, *Diplomacy*, 55; Schulzinger, *The Making of the Diplomatic Mind*, 125–126; Paul Sharp, "Who Needs Diplomats: The Problem of Diplomatic Representation," *International Journal* 52 (1997): 609–634. Diplomats are men of the world, but are not immune to prejudice. Horace Rumbold made scathing remarks directed to the national character of Poles, Turks, and Persians, among others. William Dodd had manifest prejudices, despite being a distinguished historian.
51. See also, Robert Jackson, *The Global Covenant* (Oxford: Oxford University Press, 2000), 77–96, 130–155; Eban, *Diplomacy for the Next Century*, 27–59; David Welch, "Can We Think Systematically About Ethics and Statecraft," *Ethics and International Affairs* 8 (1994): 23–37; Watson, *Diplomacy*, 66. Deceit has its limits. Diplomacy has its sensitive mechanism to detect such discreditable act.
52. Nicolson, *Diplomacy*, 109–111; Strang, *The Diplomatic Career*, 145; Callières, *The Art of Diplomacy*, 152–153, 173, 200.
53. Stanley Hoffmann, *Duties Beyond Borders* (Syracuse: Syracuse University Press, 1981), 28; Alberto R. Call, "Normative Prudence as a Tradition of Statecraft," *Ethics and International Affairs* 5 (1991): 33–51.
54. Wirtz, "Kissinger," *Diplomacy and Statecraft* 2: 109–110; Jackson, *From Anarchy to Cosmopolis*, 58–59.
55. Bozeman, *Politics and Culture*, 471–472; Callières, *The Art of Diplomacy*, 122; Nicolson, *Diplomacy*, 48, 117–118; Hoffmann, *Duties Beyond Borders*, 16; Kennan, *At Century's Ending*, 269–282.
56. Kopp and Gillespie, *Career Diplomacy*, 94–95; *Time*, September 6, 1993; Ross, *Independent Diplomat*, 15. The Department of State's venue for diplomats to voice disagreement with policy is the Dissent Channel, a forum for offering dissenting and alternative views on foreign policy.
57. Craig and George, *Force and Statecraft*, 272; Callières, *The Art of Diplomacy*, 84. "We must not form to ourselves ideas of Plato's *Republic* in the choice of persons who are designed for those kind of employment"; Herbert Butterfield, *Christianity, Diplomacy and War* (London: Epworth Press, 1953), 74; Kennan, *Memoirs*, vol. 2, 134–144; on the concept of moral minimalism see, Michael Walzer, *Thick and Thin* (Notre Dame, IN: University of Notre Dame Press, 1994), 1–19.
58. Carl E. Schorske, "Two German Ambassadors: Dirksen and Schulenburg," in Craig and Gilbert, *The Diplomats, 1919–1939*, 477–511; Franklin Ford and Carl E. Schorske, "The Voice in the Wilderness:

Robert Coulondre," ibid., 555–578; Hajo Holborn, "Diplomats and Diplomacy in the Early Weimar Republic," ibid., 123–135; David Mayers, "Neither War Nor Peace: FDR's Ambassadors in Berlin and Policy Toward Germany, 1933–1941," *Diplomacy and Statecraft* 20 (2009): 50–68.

59. Moshe Zimmermann, "Secrets and Revelations: The German Foreign Ministry and the Final Solution," *The Israel Journal of Foreign Affairs* 5 (2011): 115–123; Joschka Fischer, "Haunting Obituaries: The German Foreign Ministry's Confrontation with Its Nazi Past," ibid., 73–78.

60. In one case, a foreign officer asked for reimbursement for his travel expenses to Belgrade in October 1941, stating the aim of his trip was "liquidation of Jews in Belgrade"; *International Herald Tribune*, March 31, 2005. Joschka Fischer's decision to stop publishing obituaries for diplomats that were members of the Nazi Party has provoked a protest of German diplomats, who were guarding the reputation of "esteemed colleagues."

61. *Ha'aretz*, February 23, 2004. It is estimated that 151 diplomats have saved the life of more than 250,000 Jews during the Second World War. Among them also Hiram Bingham IV, American Deputy Consul in Marseilles, and John Cooper Wiley, American Consul in Vienna; see, Melissa J. Taylor, "Diplomats in Turmoil: Creating a Middle Ground in Post-Anschluss Austria," *Diplomatic History* 32 (2008): 811–839.

62. There are theorists who criticize the argument that diplomacy has a "liberal disposition," as diplomacy has no autonomous inclinations beyond states' policies. See also, Sharp, "Who Needs Diplomats?" *International Journal* 52: 623; "A pessimism about the human condition resides in the bosom of the best diplomats."

63. See, Mattingly, *Renaissance Diplomacy*, 45, 58; Watson, *Diplomacy*, 20; Eban, *Diplomacy for the Next Century*, 176; Adam Sisman, *A. J. P. Taylor: A Biography* (London: Mandarin, 1995), 197. Taylor's letter to the *Times* states that "appeasement is still one of the noblest words in the language in spite of its abuse twelve years ago; and appeasement should at all times be the object of an enlightened diplomacy."

64. Wight, *International Theory*, 154–156, 180, 184; Bull, *The Anarchical Society*, 167, 169, 316–317; Callières, *The Art of Diplomacy*, 170; Sharp, *Diplomatic Theory*, 39–52, 113–132; Cornelia Navari, *Internationalism and the State in the Twentieth Century* (London: Routledge, 2000), 267.

65. See, Costas M. Constantinou and James Der Derian, (eds.), *Sustainable Diplomacy* (Houndmills, UK: Palgrave Macmillan, 2010), 1–9; Reed Davis, "An Uncertain Trumpet: Reason, Anarchy and Cold War

Diplomacy in the Thought of Raymond Aron," *Review of International Studies* 34 (2008): 645–668; Jönsson and Hall, *The Essense of Diplomacy*, 33–38; Sharp, *Diplomatic Theory*, 165; Constantinou, *Human Diplomacy and Spirituality* (The Netherlands Institute of International Relations); David Wellman, *Sustainable Diplomacy: Ecology, Religion and Ethics in Muslim-Christian Relations* (New York: Palgrave Macmillan, 2004).

Chapter 8. Diplomacy Reconsidered

1. See also, Wight, *Power Politics*, 117–118; Eban, *The New Diplomacy*, 364–376; Eban, *Diplomacy for the Next Century*, 96–101.
2. Felix Gilbert, "Intellectual History: Its Aims and Method," *Daedalus* 100 (1971): 89; Der Derian, *On Diplomacy*, 4, 80; De Magalhães, *The Pure Concept of Diplomacy*, 87–95; Jönsson and Hall, *The Essence of Diplomacy*, 8–12; Constantinou, *On the Road to Diplomacy*, 47–51; Steiner, "Diplomacy and International Theory," *Review of International Studies* 30: 493–509.
3. Antony Lentin, "Several Types of Ambiguity: Lloyd George at the Paris Peace Conference," *Diplomacy and Statecraft* 6 (1995): 247.
4. See Sasson Sofer, "Old and New Diplomacy: A Debate Revisited," *Review of International Studies* 14 (1988), 195–211.
5. Grey, *Twenty-Five Years*, 277; Butterfield and Wight, *Diplomatic Investigations*, 182, 187; E. H. Carr, *The Twenty Years' Crisis, 1919–1939* (New York: Harper and Row, 1964), 17–18; Wight, *International Theory*, 199–205; Robert Tucker and David Hendrickson, "Thomas Jefferson and American Foreign Policy," *Foreign Affairs* 69 (1990): 135–156; Nicolson, *Peacemaking*, 57, 64–73.
6. Acheson, *Present at the Creation*, 727; Black, *A History of Diplomacy*, 248–263; Alan Henrikson, "Diplomacy's Possible Futures," *The Hague Journal of Diplomacy* 1 (2006): 3–27.
7. Pigman, *Contemporary Diplomacy*, 121–131; *The Hague Journal of Diplomacy, Special Issue, Rethinking the New Public Diplomacy* 2 (2007); Jan Melissen, *The New Public Diplomacy: Soft Power in International Relations* (Basingstoke, UK: Palgrave, Macmillan, 2005); Ben D. Mor, "Public Diplomacy in Grand Strategy," *Foreign Policy Analysis* 2 (2006): 157–176.
8. *New York Times*, November 29–30, 2010; Evan H. Potter, *Cyber Diplomacy* (Montreal: McGill-Queen's University Press, 2002).
9. Susan Strange, "States, Firms and Diplomacy," *International Affairs* 68 (1992): 1–15; Pigman, *Contemporary Diplomacy*, 17–7, 22–30, 70–83,

88–101; Paul Sharp, "Making Sense of Citizen Diplomats: The People of Duluth, Minnesota, as International Actors," *International Studies Perspectives* 2 (2001): 131–150; Andrew Cooper and Brian Hocking, "Governments, Non-Governmental Organizations and the Recalibration of Diplomacy," in Jönsson and Langhorne, *Diplomacy*, vol. 3, 79–95; Brian Cox and Daniel Philpott, "Faith-Based Diplomacy: An Ancient Idea Newly Emergent," *The Brandywine Review of Faith and International Affairs* (2003), 31–40; *New York Times*, October 5, 2007; *Time*, July 28, 2008. On the notion of "integrative diplomacy," see Brian Hocking, Jan Melissen, Shaun Riordan, and Paul Sharp, *Futures for Diplomacy: Integrative Diplomacy in the Twenty-First Century* (The Hague: Clingendael, Netherlands Institute of International Relations, 2012).

10. Ross, *Independent Diplomat*, 209, 203–226.
11. Sharp, *Diplomatic Theory*, 10–13, 76–78, 96.
12. Black, *A History of Diplomacy*, 248–263; Watson, *Diplomacy*, 11, 226. To a large extent diplomacy remains to be "the dialogue between independent states."
13. Robert Wolfe, "Still Lying Abroad? On the Institution of the Resident Ambassador," *Diplomacy and Statecraft* 9 (1998): 23–54; Kopp and Gillespie, *Career Diplomacy*, 113; Sharp, *Diplomatic Theory*, 293–311; Nicolson, *Diplomacy*, 38.
14. See also, Watson, *Diplomacy*, 212–227; Richard Langhorne, "Full Circle: New Principles and Old Consequences in the Modern Diplomatic System," *Diplomacy and Statecraft* 11 (2000): 33–46; Kopp and Gillespie, *Career Diplomacy*, 165–167; Hamilton and Langhorne, *The Practice of Diplomacy*, 231–245; Sharp, *Diplomatic Theory*, 222–242, 266–292; Hans Morgenthau, *Politics Among Nations* (New York: Knopf, 1973), 549.
15. Bull, *The Anarchical Society*, 173–180.

Bibliography

Acheson, Dean. *Present at the Creation: My Years at the State Department.* London: Norton, 1969.

Adcock, Frank E. and D. J. Mosley. *Diplomacy in Ancient Greece.* New York: Thomas and Hudson, 1975.

Aggestam, Karin. *Reframing and Resolving Conflict: Israel-Palestine Negotiations 1988–1998.* Lund: Lund University Press, 1999.

Algernon, Gordon Lenox (ed.). *The Dairy of Lord Bertie.* London: Hodder and Stoughton, 1924.

Alon, Ilai. *Negotiations in Arabic-Speaking Islam.* Jerusalem: The Leonard Davis Institute for International Relations, Hebrew University, 2000.

Anderson, Matthew S. *The Rise of Modern Diplomacy 1450–1919.* London: Longman, 1993.

Annan, Noel. *Our Age.* London: Weidenfeld and Nicolson, 1990.

Armitage, David. "John Locke's International Thought," in Ian Hall and Lisa Hill (eds.) *British International Thinkers from Hobbes to Namier.* New York: Palgrave, Macmillan, 2009, 33–49.

Armstrong, David. *Revolutionary Diplomacy.* Leicester, UK: Centre for the Study of Diplomacy, 1996.

Artzi, Pinhas. "The Diplomatic Service in Action: The Mittani File," in Cohen and Westbrook (eds.), *Amarna Diplomacy: The Beginnings of International Relations,* 205–211.

Baily, T. A. *The Art of Diplomacy.* New York: Meredith, 1968.

Barker, Craig J. "The Theory and Practice of Diplomatic Law in the Renaissance and Classical Periods." *Diplomacy and Statecraft* 6 (1995): 593–615.

———. *The Abuse of Diplomatic Privileges and Immunities.* Dartmouth: Aldershot, 1996.

Barston, Ronald P. *Modern Diplomacy.* London: Longman, 1988.

Berridge, G. R. "Diplomacy After Death: The Rise of the Working Funeral," *Diplomacy and Statecraft* 2 (1993): 217–234.

———. "Amarna Diplomacy: A Full-Fledged Diplomatic System?" in Cohen and Westbrook (eds.), *Amarna Diplomacy: The Beginnings of International Relations,* 212–224.

———. *Diplomacy: Theory and Practice.* Houndmills, UK: Palgrave Macmillan, 2002.

———. *Diplomatic Classics: Selected Texts from Commynes to Vattel* (Houndmills, UK: Palgrave, 2004.

Berridge, G. R. and N. Gallo. "The Role of the Diplomatic Corps: The US-North Korea Talks in Beijing, 1988–94," in Melissen (ed.), *Innovation in Diplomatic Practice,* 214–226.

Berridge, G. R., Maurice, Keens-Soper, and T. G. Otte (eds.), *Diplomatic Theory from Machiavelli to Kissinger.* Basingstoke, UK: Palgrave, 2001.

Bismarck, Otto. *The Man and the Statesman: Being the Reflections and Reminiscences of Otto von Bismarck.* London: Smith and Elder, 1898.

Black, Annabel. "The Changing Culture of Diplomatic Spouses: Some Field Notes from Brussels," *Diplomacy and Statecraft* 6 (1995): 196–222.

Black, Jeremy. *Eighteenth Century Europe.* London: Macmillan, 1999.

———. *A History of Diplomacy.* London: Reaktion Books, 2010.

Bohlen, Charles E. *Witness to History, 1929–1969.* New York: Norton, 1973.

Boyer, Mark A. "Moving Targets: Understanding Diplomacy and Negotiation in a Globalizing System." *International Studies Review* 3 (2001): 91–99.

Bozeman, Ada. *Politics and Culture in International History: From the Ancient Near East to the Opening of the Modern Age.* New Brunswick, NJ and London: Prentice Hall, 1960.

Braudel, Bernard. *A History of Civilization.* New York: Penguin, 1993.

Brecht, Bertolt. *Brecht on Theatre,* John Willet (ed.). New York: Hill and Wang, 1964.

Bridges, Peter. "On the Isthmus: A Young American at the Panama Embassy, 1959–61." *Diplomacy and Statecraft* 9 (1998): 184–197.

———. "Eugene Schuyler, the Only Diplomatist." *Diplomacy and Statecraft* 16 (2005): 13–22.

Britton, Roswell. "Chinese Interstate Intercourse Before 700 B.C.," in Jönsson and Langhorne (eds.), *Diplomacy,* vol. 2, 91–111.

Bull, Headly. *The Anarchical Society.* London: Macmillan, 1982.

———, Benedict Kingsbury, and Adam Roberts (eds.). *Hugo Grotius and International Relations.* Oxford: Oxford University Press, 1992.

Busk, Douglas, *The Craft of Diplomacy.* London: Paul Mall, 1967.

Butterfield, Herbert. *Christianity, Diplomacy and War.* London: Epworth Press, 1953.

———. "The New Diplomacy and Historical Diplomacy," in Butterfield and Wight (eds.), *Diplomatic Investigations*, 181–192.

———. "The Balance of Power," in Butterfield and Wight (eds.), *Diplomatic Investigations*, 132–148.

Butterfield, Herbert and Martin Wight (eds.). *Diplomatic Investigations.* London: George Allen and Unwin, 1966.

Bylica, Jacek. "My Years with Gorbachev and Shevardnadze: A Memoir of a Soviet Interpreter by Pavel Palazchenko." *The Fletcher Forum of World Affairs* 22 (1998): 149–155.

Call, Alberto R. "Normative Prudence as a Tradition of Statecraft." *Ethics and International Affairs* 5 (1991): 33–51.

De Callières, François, Maurice A. Keens-Soper, and Karl W. Schweizer, (eds.). *The Art of Diplomacy.* Leicester, UK: Leicester University Press, New York: Holmes and Maier, 1983.

Cameron, Elizabeth. "Alexis Saint-Léger," in Craig and Gilbert (eds.), *The Diplomats 1919–1939*, 376–405.

Campbell, Brian. "Diplomacy in the Roman World (c. 500 B.C.–A.D. 235)," *Diplomacy and Statecraft* 12 (2001): 1–22.

Carr, E. H. *The Twenty Years Crisis, 1919–1939.* New York: Harper and Row, 1964.

Carter, Charles H. "The Ambassadors of Early Modern Europe: Patterns of Diplomatic Representation in the Early Seventeenth Century," in Jönsson and Langhorne (eds.), *Diplomacy*, vol. 2, 232–250.

Clark, Eric. *Corps Diplomatique.* London: A. Lane, 1973.

Clarke, John. *British Diplomacy and Foreign Policy, 1782–1865.* London: Unwin Hyman, 1989.

Clinton, David. "Emotion and Calculation: Callières and Bismarck." Paper presented at the International Studies Association Convention, Montreal, March 2004.

Cohen, Raymond. *The Theatre of Power.* London: Longman, 1987.

———. *Negotiations Across Cultures.* Washington DC: United States Institute of Peace Press, 1991.

———. "All in the Family: Ancient Near Eastern Diplomacy," *International Negotiation* 1 (1996): 11–28.

———. *International Negotiations: A Semantic Analysis.* Leicester, UK: University of Leicester, Centre for the Study of Diplomacy, 1999.

———. "Reflections on the New Global Diplomacy: Statecraft from 2500 B.C. to 2000 A.D.," in Melissen (ed.), *Innovation in Diplomatic Practice*, 1–18.

————. "Meaning, Interpretation and International Negotiation," *Global Society* 14 (2000): 317–335.

————. "The Great Tradition: The Spread of Diplomacy in the Ancient World." *Diplomacy and Statecraft* 12 (2001): 23–38.

————. "Language and Conflict Resolution: The Limits of English." *International Studies Review* 3 (2001): 25–51.

Cohen, Raymond and Raymond Westbrook (eds.). *Amarna Diplomacy: The Beginnings of International Relations.* Baltimore: Johns Hopkins University Press, 1999.

Collier, Peter and David Horowitz. *The Kennedys.* New York: Warner, 1984.

Constantinou, Costas M. "Diplomatic Representations . . . Or Who Framed the Ambassadors?" *Millennium* 23 (1994): 1–23.

————. *States of Political Discourse: Words, Regimes, Seditions* (London: Routledge, 2004).

————. *Human Diplomacy and Spirituality.* Clingendael: Netherlands Institute of International Relations, 2006.

Constantinou, Costas M. and James Der Derian (eds.). *Sustainable Diplomacy.* Houndmills, UK: Palgrave Macmillan, 2010.

Constantinou, Costas M., Oliver Richmond, and Alison Watson. "International Relations and the Challenges of Global Communication." *Review of International Studies* 34 (2008): 1–19.

Cooper, Andrew and Brian Hocking. "Governments, Non-Governmental Organizations and the Recalibration of Diplomacy," in Jönsson and Langhorne (eds.), *Diplomacy,* vol. 3, 79–95.

Corbett, Theodor. "The Cult of Lipsius: A Leading Source of Early Modern Spanish Statecraft." *Journal of the History of Ideas* 36 (1975): 139–152.

Corp, Edward. "Sir Eyre Crowe and George Clemenceau at the Paris Peace Conference, 1919–1920." *Diplomacy and Statecraft* 8 (1997): 10–19.

Cox, Brian and Daniel Philpott. "Faith-Based Diplomacy: An Ancient Idea Newly Emergent." *The Brandywine Review of Faith and International Affairs* (2003): 31–40.

Craig, Gordon A. and Alexander George. *Force and Statecraft.* Oxford: Oxford University Press, 1982.

Craig, Gordon A. and Felix Gilbert (eds.). *The Diplomats, 1919–1939.* New York: Atheneum, 1968.

Craig, Gordon A. and Francis Loewenheim. *The Diplomats, 1939–1979.* Princeton: Princeton University Press, 1994.

Crawford, C. Neta. "The Passion of World Politics." *International Security,* 24 (2000): 116–156.

Cuttino, G. P. *English Medieval Diplomacy*. Bloomington: Indiana University Press, 1985.

Dallek, Robert. *John F. Kennedy: An Unfinished Life 1917–1963*. London: Penguin, 2004.

Davetak, Richard. "Discipline and Balance: Vattel and the Birth of International Relations Theory." Paper presented at the International Studies Association Convention, Washington DC, February 1999.

Davis, Reed. "An Uncertain Trumpet: Reason, Anarchy and Cold War Diplomacy in the Thought of Raymond Aron." *Review of International Studies* 34 (2008): 645–668.

De Grazia, Sebastian. *Machiavelli in Hell*. New York: Vintage Books, 1994.

De Madaraiga, Salvador. *Englishmen, Frenchmen, Spaniards*. Oxford: Oxford University Press, 1928.

De Magalhães, José Calvert. *The Pure Concept of Diplomacy*. New York: Greenwood Press, 1988.

Der Derian, James. *On Diplomacy*. Oxford: Blackwell, 1987.

———. *Antidiplomacy: Spies, Terror, Speed and War*. Oxford: Oxford University Press, 1992.

Deshingkar, Giri. "Strategic Thinking in Ancient India and China: Kautilya and Sunzi," in Jönsson and Langhorne (eds.), *Diplomacy* vol. 2, 79–90.

Dixon, Piers. *Double Diploma*. London: Hutchinson, 1968.

Donald, David H., *Lincoln*. London: Jonathan Cape, 1995.

Dunn, David (ed.). *Diplomacy at the Highest Level*. Basingstoke: Macmillan, 1996.

Eayrs, James. *Diplomacy and Its Discontents* (Toronto: University of Toronto Press, 1971).

Eban, Abba. *An Autobiography*. New York: Random House, 1977.

———. *The New Diplomacy*. New York: Random House, 1983.

———. *Diplomacy for the Next Century*. New Haven: Yale University Press, 1998.

Eden, Anthony. *Full Circle: The Memoirs of Lord Avon*. London: Cassell, 1960.

Eilts, F. "Diplomacy—Contemporary Practice," in Plischke, *Modern Diplomacy*, 3–18.

Elias, Norbert. *The Civilizing Process*. Oxford: Blackwell, 1982.

———. *The Court Society*. Oxford: Blackwell, 1983.

Enloe, Cynthia. *Bananas, Beaches and Bases*. Albany: State University of New York Press, 1990.

Feinstein, Adam. *Pablo Neruda*. London: Bloomsbury, 2004.

Feltham, Ralph G. *Diplomatic Handbook*. London: Longman, 1970.

Fischer, Joschka. "Haunting Obituaries: The German Foreign Ministry's Confrontation with Its Nazi Past," *Israel Journal of Foreign Affairs* 5 (2011): 73–78.

Ford, Franklin and Carl E. Schorske. "The Voice in Wilderness: Robert Coulondre," in Craig and Gilbert (eds.), *The Diplomats, 1919–1939*, 555–578.

Fraser, Antonia. *King Charles II*. London: Phoenix, 1979.

Freeman, Chas. "Lingua Diplomatica." *Foreign Policy* (November-December, 2002): 84–88.

Frey, Linda and Marsha Frey. "International Officials and the Standard of Diplomatic Privilege." *Diplomacy and Statecraft* 9 (1998): 1–17.

———. *The History of Diplomatic Immunity*. Columbus: Ohio State University Press, 1999.

Gaddis, John. "Rescuing Choice from Circumstance: The Statecraft of Henry Kissinger," in Craig and Loewenheim (eds.), *The Diplomats, 1939–1979*, 1994, 564–592.

Galtung, Johan and Mari Holmboe Ruge. "Patterns of Diplomacy: A Study of Recruitment and Career Patterns in Norwegian Diplomacy," *Journal of Peace Research* 2 (1965): 101–135,

Gilbert, Felix. "The 'New Diplomacy' of the Eighteenth Century." *World Politics* 4 (1951): 1–38.

———. *To the Farewell Address: The Beginning of American Foreign Policy*. New York: Harper and Row, 1965.

———. "Intellectual History: Its Aims and Method." *Daedalus* 100 (1971): 80–97.

Gilbert, Martin. *Sir Horace Rumbold*. London: Heinemann, 1973.

Gilboa, Eytan. "Diplomacy in the Media Age: Three Models of Uses and Effects." *Diplomacy and Statecraft* 12 (2001): 1–28.

Goffman, Erving. *Behavior in Public Places*. New York: The Free Press, 1963.

———. *Interaction Ritual*. Chicago: Aldine, 1967.

Goldstein, Erik. "The Politics of the State Visit." *Diplomacy and Statecraft* 12 (2001): 1–28.

———. "The Origins of Summit Diplomacy," in Dunn (ed.), *Diplomacy at the Highest Level*, 23–37.

Grew, Joseph C. and E. Johnson (ed.). *Turbulent Era*. London: Hammond, 1953.

Grey, Edward. *Twenty-Five Years, 1892–1916*. New York: F. A. Stokes, 1925.

Gurevitch, Z. D. "Distance and Conversation." *Symbolic Interactions* 12 (1989): 251–263.

———. "The Power of Not Understanding: The Meeting of Conflicting Identities," *Journal of Applied Behavioral Science* 25 (1989): 161–173.

Hamilton, Keith and Richard Langhorne. *The Practice of Diplomacy.* London: Routledge, 1995.

Hardinge of Penshurst, Lord. *Old Diplomacy.* London: John Murray, 1947.

Hardy, Michael. *Modern Diplomatic Law.* Manchester: Manchester University Press, 1968.

Hare, Paul and Herbert Blumberg (eds.). *Dramaturgical Analysis of Social Interaction.* New York: Praeger, 1987.

Harmon, Robert. *The Art and Practice of Diplomacy.* Scarecrow: Metuchen, 1971.

Harr, John E. *The Professional Diplomat.* Princeton: Princeton University Press, 1969.

Harriman, Averell (and Elie Abel). *Special Envoy to Churchill and Stalin, 1941–1946.* New York: Random House, 1975.

Harris, Brian. "Ernest Satow's Early Career as Diplomatic Interpreter." *Diplomacy and Statecraft* 13 (2002): 116–134.

Hemery, John. "Educating Diplomats." *International Studies Perspectives* 3 (2002): 140–145.

Henderson, Nevile. *Water Under the Bridges.* London: Hodder and Stoughton, 1945.

Henderson, Nicholas. "The Washington Embassy: Navigating the Waters of the Potomac." *Diplomacy and Statecraft* 1 (1990): 40–48.

Henrikson, Alan. "Diplomacy's Possible Futures." *The Hague Journal of Diplomacy* 1 (2006): 3–27.

Hickman, Katie. *Daughters of Britannia: The Lives and Times of Diplomatic Wives.* London: Flamingo, 2000.

History Notes. Women in Diplomacy. The FCO, 1782–1994. London: History Branch, LRD no. 6, 1994.

Hocking, Brian. *Beyond "Newness" and "Decline": The Development of Catalytic Diplomacy.* Leicester, UK: University of Leicester, Centre for the Study of Diplomacy, 1995.

Hocking, Brian, Jan Melissen, Shaun Riordan, and Paul Sharp. *Futures for Diplomacy: Integrative Diplomacy in the Twenty-First Century.* The Hague: Clingendael, Netherlands Institute for International Relations, 2012.

Hoffman, John. "Reconstructing Diplomacy." *British Journal of Politics and International Relations* 5 (2003): 525–542.

Hoffmann, Stanley. *Duties Beyond Borders.* Syracuse: Syracuse University Press, 1981.

Holborn, Hajo. "Diplomats and Diplomacy in the Early Weimar Republic," in Craig and Gilbert (eds.), *The Diplomats, 1919–1939*, 123–135.

Holsti, Kalevi. *International Politics: A Framework for Analysis.* Englewood Cliffs, NJ: Prentice Hall, 1992.

Hugill, Peter. *Global Communications Since 1944: Geopolitics and Technology.* Baltimore: The Johns Hopkins University Press, 1999.

Hurrell, Andrew. "Headly Bull and Diplomacy." Paper presented at the International Studies Association Convention, New Orleans, March 2002.

Jackson, Robert. *The Global Covenant.* Oxford: Oxford University Press, 2000.

———. *Classical and Modern Thought on International Relations: From Anarchy to Cosmopolis.* New York: Palgrave Macmillan, 2005.

James, Alan. "Diplomacy and International Society." *International Relations* 6 (1980): 931–948.

———. "Diplomacy." *Review of International Studies* 19 (1993): 91–100.

Jeffrey, Renée. *Hugo Grotius in International Relations.* Harmondsworth, UK: Palgrave Macmillan, 2006.

Jones, Dorothy V. *Splendid Encounters: The Thought and Conduct of Diplomacy.* Chicago: University of Chicago Library, 1984.

Jönsson, Christer. "Diplomatic Signaling in the Television Age," in Jönsson and Langhorne, *Diplomacy,* vol. 3, 120–134.

Jönsson, Christer and Martin Hall. "Communication: An Essential Aspect of Diplomacy." *International Studies Perspectives* 4 (2003): 195–210.

———. *Essence of Diplomacy.* London: Palgrave Macmillan, 2005.

Jönsson, Christer and Richard Langhorne (eds.). *Diplomacy.* London: Sage, 2004.

Kaufman, Johan. *Conference Diplomacy.* London: Macmillan, 1996.

Kaufman, William. "The American Ambassadors: Bullitt and Kennedy," in Craig and Gilbert (eds.), *The Diplomats, 1919–1939,* 649–681.

Keens-Soper, Maurice. "The Liberal Disposition of Diplomacy." *International Relations* 2 (1973): 907–917.

———. "Abraham de Wicquefort and Diplomatic Theory." *Diplomacy and Statecraft* 8 (1997): 16–30.

Kelly, David. *The Ruling Few.* London: Hollis and Carter, 1952.

Kennan, George F. *Memoirs, 1925–1950.* Boston: Little and Brown, 1967.

———. *Memoirs, 1950–1963.* Boston: Little and Brown, 1972.

———. *At Century's Ending.* New York: Norton, 1996.

———. "Diplomacy Without Diplomats." *Foreign Affairs* 76 (1997): 199–211.

Kertzer, David. *Ritual, Politics and Power.* New Haven: Yale University Press, 1988.

Kirkpatrick, Ivone. *The Inner Circle.* London: Macmillan, 1959.

Kissinger, Henry. *A World Restored.* Boston: Houghton Mifflin, 1957.

———. "The White Revolutionary: Reflections on Bismarck." *Daedalus* 97 (1968): 888–924.

———. *The White House Years.* London: Weidenfeld and Nicolson, 1979.

———. *Diplomacy.* New York: Simon and Schuster, 1994.

Kleiman, Aharon. *Constructive Ambiguity in Middle-East Peace-Making.* Tel Aviv: The Tami Steinmetz Center for Peace Research, 1999.

Knecht, Robert. *Richelieu.* London: Longman, 1991.

Kopp, Harry and Charles Gillespie. *Career Diplomacy: Life and Work in the United States Foreign Service.* Washington, DC: Georgetown University Press, 2008.

Kurbalija, Jovan. "Diplomacy in the Age of Information Technology," in Melissen (ed.), *Innovation in Diplomatic Practice,* 171–189.

Kurbalija, Jovan and Hanna Slavik (eds.). *Language and Diplomacy.* Malta: Mediterranean Academy of Diplomatic Studies, 2001.

Lafont, Bertrand. "International Relations in the Ancient Near East: The Birth of a Complete Diplomatic System." *Diplomacy and Statecraft* 12 (2001): 39–60.

Langhorne, Richard. "The Regulation of Diplomatic Practice: The Beginnings to the Vienna Convention on Diplomatic Relations, 1961." *Review of International Studies* 18 (1992): 3–17.

———. "Current Developments in Diplomacy: Who Are the Diplomats Now?" *Diplomacy and Statecraft* 8 (1997): 1–15.

———. "Full Circle: New Principles and Old Consequences in the Modern Diplomatic System." *Diplomacy and Statecraft* 11 (2000): 33–46.

Lauren, Paul G. *Diplomats and Bureaucrats.* Palo Alto: Stanford University Press, 1976.

Lawford, Valentine. *Bound for Diplomacy.* London: John Murray, 1963.

Lee, Dona. "The Growing Influence of Business in United Kingdom Diplomacy." *International Studies Perspectives* 5 (2004): 50–65.

Lee, Dona and David Hudson. "The Old and New Significance of Political Economy and Diplomacy." *Review of International Studies* 30 (2004): 343–360.

Lee, Michael. "British Cultural Diplomacy and the Cold War: 1946–1961." *Diplomacy and Statecraft* 9 (1998): 112–134.

Leguey-Feilleux, Jean-Robert. *The Dynamics of Diplomacy.* Boulder: Lynn Rienner, 2009.

Leibniz, Gottfried Wilhelm, edited by Patrick Riley. *Leibniz, Political Writings.* Cambridge, UK: Cambridge University Press, 1988.

Leira, Halvard. "Justus Lipsius, Political Humanism and the Disciplining of Seventeenth Century Statecraft." *Review of International Study* 34 (2008): 669–692.

Lentin, Antony. "Several Types of Ambiguity: Lloyd George at the Paris Peace Conference." *Diplomacy and Statecraft* 6 (1995): 223–251.

Little, Douglas. "Crackpot Realists and Other Heroes: The Rise and Fall of the Post-War American Diplomatic Elite." *Diplomacy and Statecraft* 13 (2002): 99–112.

Liverani, Mario. *International Relations in the Ancient Near East, 1600–1100 B.C.* Houndmills, UK: Palgrave, 2001.

———. "The Great Powers Club," in Cohen and Westbrook (eds.), *Amarna Diplomacy: The Beginnings of International Relations*, 15–27.

Lloyd, Lorna. "Diplomats: A Breed Apart or Anyone Goes? The Question of Political Appointees as Head of Missions," Paper presented at the Annual Convention of the International Studies Association, San Diego, March 2006.

Machiavelli, Nicolò. *The Prince*. New York: Norton, 1977.

Macomber, William B. *The Angels' Game: A Handbook of Modern Diplomacy.* London: Longman, 1975.

Mallett, Michael. "Italian Renaissance Diplomacy." *Diplomacy and Statecraft* 12 (2001): 61–70.

Mastenbreak, Willem. "Negotiation as Emotion Management." *Theory, Culture and Society* 16 (1999): 49–73.

Mattingly, Garrett. *Renaissance Diplomacy*. Harmondsworth, UK: Penguin, 1966.

Mayers, David. "Neither War Nor Peace: FDR's Ambassadors in Berlin and Policy Toward Germany, 1933–1941." *Diplomacy and Statecraft* 20 (2009): 50–68.

McDermott, Geoffrey. *The New Diplomacy*. London: Plume Press, 1973.

McDonald, John. *How to Be a Delegate: International Conference Diplomacy.* Washington DC: The Institute for Multi-Track Diplomacy, 1994.

McKercher, B. J. C. "The Last Old Diplomat: Sir Robert Vansittart and the Verities of British Foreign Policy, 1903–1930." *Diplomacy and Statecraft* 6 (1995): 1–38.

McLean, Roderick R. *Royalty and Diplomacy in Europe, 1890–1914.* Cambridge: Cambridge University Press, 2001.

Meers, Paul. "The Changing Nature of Diplomatic Negotiation," in Melissen (ed.), *Innovation in Diplomatic Practice:* 79–92.

Melissen, Jan. *Innovation in Diplomatic Practice*. Basingstoke, UK: Palgrave, Macmillan, 1999.

———. *The New Public Diplomacy: Soft Power in International Relations.* Basingstoke, UK: Palgrave, Macmillan, 2005.

Miller, Robert H. *Inside an Embassy: The Political Role of Diplomats Abroad.* Washington, DC: Institute for the Study of Diplomacy, 1992.

Mor, Ben D. "Public Diplomacy in Grand Strategy." *Foreign Policy Analysis* 2 (2006): 157–176.

Morgenthau, Hans. *Politics Among Nations*. New York: Knopf, 1973.

Mosley, Leonard. *Curzon.* London: Longmans and Greene, 1961.

Mowat, Robert B. *Diplomacy and Peace.* London: Williams and Norgate, 1935.

Mukerji, Girija K. *Diplomacy: Theory and History.* New Delhi: Trimurti, 1973.

Munck, Thomas. *Seventeenth Century Europe, 1598–1700.* London: Macmillan, 1990.

Muir, Edward. *Ritual in Early Modern Europe.* Cambridge: Cambridge University Press, 1997.

Munn-Rankin, Joan. "Diplomacy in Western Asia in the Early Second Millennium B.C.," in Jönsson and Langhorne (eds.), *Diplomacy,* vol. 2, 1–43.

Murray, Stuart. "Consolidating the Gains Made in Diplomatic Studies: A Taxonomy." *International Studies Perspectives* 9 (2008): 22–39.

Nash, Philip. "A Woman's Touch in Foreign Affairs? The Career of Ambassador Frances E. Willis." *Diplomacy and Statecraft* 13 (2002): 1–20.

———. "America's First Female Chief of Mission: Ruth Bryan Owen, Minister to Denmark, 1933–36." *Diplomacy and Statecraft* 16 (2005): 52–72.

Navari, Cornelia. *Internationalism and the State in the Twentieth Century.* London: Routledge, 2000.

Neruda, Pablo. *Memoirs.* Harmondsworth: Penguin, 1982.

Neumann, Iver B. "Self and Other in International Relations." *European Journal of International Relations* 2 (1996): 139–174.

———. "Returning Practice to the Linguistic Turn: The Case of Diplomacy." *Millennium* 31 (2002): 627–651.

———. "The Body of the Diplomat." *European Journal of International Relations* 14 (2008): 671–695.

———. "Sublime Diplomacy: Byzantine, Early Modern, Contemporary." *Millennium* 34 (2006): 865–888.

———. "A Speech that the Entire Ministry May Stand For: Or, Why Diplomats Never Produce Anything New." *International Political Sociology* 1 (2007): 183–200.

Nicolson, Harold. *Peacemaking, 1919.* London: Constable, 1933.

Obolensky, Dimitri. "The Principles and Methods of Byzantine Diplomacy," in Jönsson and Langhorne (eds.), *Diplomacy,* vol. 2, 112–129.

Orebaugh, Walter (with Carol Jose). *The Consul.* Cape Canaveral: Blue Note, 1994.

Oren, Nissan. "Statecraft and the Academic Intellectual," in Idem (ed.), *Intellectuals in Politics.* Jerusalem: The Magnes Press, 1984, 9–14.

Otte, T. G. "'Not Proficient in Table-Thumbing': Sir Ernest Satow in Peking, 1900–1906." *Diplomacy and Statecraft* 13 (2002): 161–200.

————. "A Manual of Diplomacy: The Genesis of Satow's Guide to Diplomatic Practice." *Diplomacy and Statecraft* 13 (2002): 229–243.

Panikkar, Kavalam Madh. *The Principles and Practice of Diplomacy*. Bombay: Asia, 1956.

Pigman, Geoffrey A. *Contemporary Diplomacy*. Cambridge, UK: Polity, 2010.

Plischke, Elmer (ed.). *Modern Diplomacy: The Art and the Artisans*. Washington, DC: American Enterprise Institute of Public Research, 1975.

————. *United States Department of State*. Westport: Greenwood Press, 1999.

Potter, Evan H. *The Office of Ambassador in the Middle Ages*. Princeton: Princeton University Press, 1967.

————. *Cyber Diplomacy*. Montreal: McGill-Queen's University Press, 2002.

————. *Canada and the New Public Diplomacy*. Clingendael: The Netherlands Institute of International Relations, 2002.

————. "Branding Canada: Renaissance of Canada's Commercial Diplomacy." *International Studies Perspectives* 5 (2004): 55–60.

Queller, Donald E. *Early Venetian Legislation on Ambassadors*. Geneva: Librairie Droz, 1966.

————. *The Office of Ambassador in the Middle Ages*. Princeton: Princeton University Press, 1967.

————. "Medieval Diplomacy," in Jönsson and Langhorne (eds.), *Diplomacy*, vol. 2, 193–213.

Ramaswamy, T. N. (ed.). *Essentials of Indian Statecraft: Kautilya's Arthashastra for Contemporary Readers*. London: Asia, 1962.

Rangarajan, L. N. "Diplomacy, States and Secrecy in Communication." *Diplomacy and Statecraft* 9 (1998): 18–49.

Rangarajan, L. "Classical Indian Diplomacy." Paper presented at the Conference on the 350th Anniversary of the Peace of Westphalia, Enschede, The Netherlands, July 1998.

Rawnsley, Gary. *Radio Diplomacy and Propaganda: The BBC and VOA in International Politics, 1956–1964*. London: Macmillan, 1996.

Regionieri, Rodolfo. "The Amarna Age: International Society in the Making," in Cohen and Westbrook (eds.), *Amarna Diplomacy: The Beginning of International Relations*, 42–53.

Rendel, George. *The Sword and the Olive*. London: John Murray, 1957.

Reus-Smit, Christian. *The Moral Purpose of the State*. Princeton: Princeton University Press, 1999.

Roberts, Andrew. *The Holy Fox: Biography of Lord Halifax*. London: Weidenfeld and Nicolson, 1991.

Rose, Norman. *Vansittart: A Study of a Diplomat*. London: Heinemann, 1978.

————. *Harold Nicolson: A Curious and Colorful Life.* London: Jonathan Cape, 2005.

Ross, Carne. *Independent Diplomat: Dispatches from an Unaccountable Elite.* Ithaca, NY: Cornell University Press, 2007.

Ross, George Macdonald. *Leibniz.* Oxford: Oxford University Press, 1984.

Satow, Ernest. *A Guide to Diplomatic Practice.* London: Longman, Green and Co., 1922.

Schlesinger, Arthur. *A Thousand Days: John F. Kennedy at the White House.* Boston: Houghton Mifflin, 1965.

Schorske, Carl E. "Two German Ambassadors: Dirksen and Schulenburg," in Craig and Gilbert, *The Diplomats, 1919–1939,* 477–511.

Schuetz, Alfred. "The Stranger: An Essay in Social Psychology," *The American Journal of Sociology* 49 (1944): 499–507.

Schulzinger, Robert. *The Making of the Diplomatic Mind.* Middletown, CN: Wesleyan University Press, 1975.

Searle, John. *The Construction of Social Reality.* London: Penguin, 1995.

Sharp, Paul. "Who Needs Diplomats: The Problem of Diplomatic Representation." *International Journal* 52 (1997): 609–634.

————. "For Diplomacy: Representation and the Study of International Relations." *International Studies Review* 1 (1999): 33–57.

————. "Making Sense of Citizen Diplomats: The People of Duluth, Minnesota, as International Actors." *International Studies Perspectives* 2 (2001): 131–150.

————. *The English School, Herbert Butterfield and Diplomacy.* Clingendael: Netherlands Institute of International Relations, 2002.

————. *Diplomatic Theory of International Relations.* Cambridge: Cambridge University Press, 2009.

Sharp, Paul and Geoffrey Wiseman (eds.). *The Diplomatic Corps as an Institution of International Society.* Houndmills. UK: Palgrave Macmillan, 2007.

Shephard, Jonathan. "Information, Disinformation and Delay in Byzantine Diplomacy," in Jönsson and Langhorne (eds.), *Diplomacy*, vol. 2, 130–174.

Simmel, Georg. "The Stranger," in *Georg Simmel on Individuality and Social Forms*, Donald Levine (ed.) Chicago: University of Chicago Press, 1972.

Siracusa, Joseph M. *Diplomacy: A Very Short Introduction.* Oxford: Oxford University Press, 2010.

Sisman, Adam. *A. J. P. Taylor: A Biography* (London: Mandarin, 1995).

Smith, Jean E. *FDR.* New York: Random House, 2007.

Sofer, Sasson. "Old and New Diplomacy: A Debate Revisited." *Review of International Studies* 14 (1988): 195–211.

Sorensen, Ted. *The Counselor.* New York: Harper Perennial, 2008.

Stearns, Monteagle. *Talking to Strangers.* Princeton: Princeton University Press, 1996.

Steiner, Barry. "Diplomacy and International Theory." *Review of International Studies* 30 (2004): 492–509.

Steiner, Zara S. *The Foreign Office and Foreign Policy 1898–1914.* Cambridge: Cambridge University Press, 1969.

Stone, Lawrence. *The Crisis of the Aristocracy, 1558–1641.* Oxford: Oxford University Press, 1965.

Strang, William. *The Diplomatic Career.* London: Andre Deutsch, 1962.

Strange, Susan. "States, Firms and Diplomacy," *International Affairs* 68 (1992): 1–15.

Sullivan, Joseph (ed.). *Embassies Under Siege.* Washington, DC: Brassey's, 1995.

Sutlive, Vinson, Nathan Altshuler, and Mario Zamora (eds.). *Anthropological Diplomacy: Issues and Principles.* Williamsburg: College of William and Mary, 1982.

Taylor, A. J. P. *Bismarck: The Man and the Statesman.* New York: Alfred A. Knopf, 1955.

———. *Europe: Grandeur and Decline.* Harmondsworth: Penguin, 1967.

———. *The Struggle for Mastery in Europe.* London: Oxford University Press, 1971.

Taylor, Melissa J. "Diplomats in Turmoil: Creating a Middle Ground in Post-Anschluss Austria," *Diplomatic History* 32 (2008): 811–839.

Thayer, Charles W. "Procedure and Protocol," in Plischke (ed.), *Modern Diplomacy: The Art and the Artisans*, 389–402.

Thomas, Evan. *Robert Kennedy.* New York: Simon and Schuster, 2000.

Tolstoy, Leo. *Anna Karenina.* Mineola, NY: Dover, 2004.

Tuck, Richard. *The Rights of War and Peace.* Oxford: Oxford University Press, 1999.

Tucker, Robert and David Hendrickson. "Thomas Jefferson and American Foreign Policy." *Foreign Affairs* 69 (1990): 135–156.

Vagts, Alfred. *Defense and Diplomacy.* New York: King's Crown Press, 1956.

Vansittart, Robert. *Collected Poems.* London: Lavat Dickson, 1934.

Walzer, Michael. *Thick and Thin* (Notre Dame, IN: Notre Dame University Press, 1994).

Watson, Adam. *Diplomacy: The Dialogue Between States.* New York: New Press, 1983.

Wedgwood, Veronica C. *The Thirty Years Crisis.* London: Jonathan Cape, 1968.

Welch, David. "Can We Think Systematically About Ethics and Statecraft." *Ethics and International Affairs* 8 (1994): 23–37.

Wellesley, Victor. *Diplomacy in Fetters*. London: Hutchinson, 1944.

Wellman, David. *Sustainable Diplomacy: Ecology, Religion and Ethics in Muslim-Christian Relations*. New York: Palgrave Macmillan, 2004.

Wight, Martin. *Systems of States*. Leicester, UK: Leicester University Press, 1977.

———. *Power Politics*, 2nd ed. Harmondsworth, UK: Penguin and the Royal Institute of International Relations, 1986.

———. *International Theory: The Three Traditions*. Wight, Gabriel and Brian Porter(eds.). Leicester, UK: Leicester University Press, 1991.

Wirtz, Richard. "Henry Kissinger's Philosophy of International Relations," *Diplomacy and Statecraft* 2 (1991): 103–129.

Wiseman, Geoffrey. "Adam Watson on Diplomacy." Paper presented at the International Studies Association Convention, New Orleans, March 2002.

———. "Pax Americana: Bumping into Diplomatic Culture." *International Studies Perspectives* 6 (2005): 409–430.

Wolfe, Robert. "Still Lying Abroad? On the Institution of the Resident Ambassador." *Diplomacy and Statecraft* 9 (1998): 23–54.

Wolff, Kurt H. (ed.). *The Sociology of Georg Simmel*. New York: The Free Press, 1950.

———. (ed.). *Georg Simmel, 1858–1918*. Columbus: Ohio State University Press, 1955.

Wolpert, Andrew. "The Genealogy of Diplomacy in Classical Greece." *Diplomacy and Statecraft* 12 (2001): 71–88.

Wood, John and Jean Serres. *Diplomatic Ceremonial and Protocol: Principles, Procedures and Practices*. New York: Columbia University Press, 1970.

Woolf, Virginia. *Orlando*. Harmondsworth, UK: Penguin, 1993.

Zartman, William. *Negotiations as a Mechanism for Resolution in the Arab-Israeli Conflict*. Jerusalem: The Leonard Davis Institute for International Relations, 1999.

Zimmermann, Moshe. "Secrets and Revelations: The German Foreign Ministry and the Final Solution." *Israel Journal of Foreign Affairs* 5 (2011): 115–123.

Index

121